THE BEST BET

THE BEST BET

Forming the Right Relationships
and
Making the Most of your Relationship

BASED ON
TRADITIONAL VEDIC ASTROLOGICAL TECHNICS
ADAPTED TO MODERN MATRIMONIAL POLEMICS

K. JAYA SEKHAR

MOTILAL BANARSIDASS PUBLISHERS
PRIVATE LIMITED • DELHI

First Published: 2002

ISBN: 81-208-1878-4 (Cloth)
ISBN: 81-208-1882-2 (Paper)

Also available at:

MOTILAL BANARSIDASS

41 U.A. Bungalow Road, Jawahar Nagar, Delhi 110 007
8 Mahalaxmi Chambers, 22 Bhulabhai Desai Road, Mumbai 400 026
236, 9th Main III Block, Jayanagar, Bangalore 560 011
120 Royapettah High Road, Mylapore, Chennai 600 004
Sanas Plaza, 1302 Baji Rao Road, Pune 411 002
8 Camac Street, Kolkata 700 017
Ashok Rajpath, Patna 800 004
Chowk, Varanasi 221 001

Printed in India

BY JAINENDRA PRAKASH JAIN AT SHRI JAINENDRA PRESS,
A-45 NARAINA, PHASE-I, NEW DELHI 110 028
AND PUBLISHED BY NARENDRA PRAKASH JAIN FOR
MOTILAL BANARSIDASS PUBLISHERS PRIVATE LIMITED,
BUNGALOW ROAD, DELHI 110 007

To
My Dad
But For Whom
I Would Have Been
An Obscure Happy Painter!

Contents

Vedic Verses

* I worship SHIVA, who spreads fragrance and blesses me with a husband. May He release me from the parent's home, like a ripe fruit from the stem and never release me from the husband's home.

(Prayer of a maiden : Yajur Veda 3-60)

* I am the Sama (song): You are Rik (Verse)
I am Purusha (Heaven); you are Prakriti (Earth)
We together will live here, becoming parents of children.

(Prayer of a groom : Atharva Veda xiv. 2-71)

* Join us as a couple, Indra, in the strongest bonds of love, like the chakravaka bird and its mate, Oh! Gods, unite us both by joining our hearts together.

(Prayer by the bride and groom Atharva Veda xiv. 2-64. Rig Veda x 85-47)

* May you together enjoy prosperity, fortune, conducting yourselves according to Dharma (Duty); hoping for love; children; husband and wife being of one mind; enjoy the full term of life; then growing old together worship for immortality.

(Blessings of the priests)

* *Free translation from the original Sanskrit.*

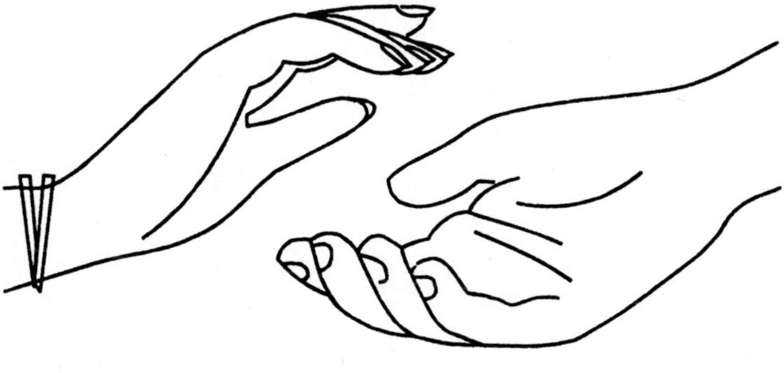

Preface

Almost immediately after completing my college education I *declared* myself a professional astrologer. The choice of the profession was made more for reason of birth to a famous and successful astrologer than by virtue of any serious conviction in astrology or attraction to the subject. At heart I longed to be an artist. In fact I should confess that I was more skeptical about the subject than some of my friends.

However, I honestly applied the rules I had learnt and gave my readings. As the years rolled by I found the rules worked. When the predictions came true I was more surprised than my unbelieving clients. Today I carry on my profession with real conviction. But, to be honest, somewhere in the recesses of my mind there lies an element of skepticism. That is why in spite of my great reverence and admiration for the works of ancient Hindu sages, it is hard for me to unquestioningly accept any rules, as though they were religious doctrines. I try to analyze, find the truth, the logic, and the rationale behind them and reject those that are apparently irrelevant in the modern context.

It is well-known that the ancient Hindu sages never divulged the logic or the process by which they evolved the rules. But if we knew their reasoning and methodology, it could help us to apply the rules in the proper spirit in which they were meant to be used. We would also succeed in dismantling several subsequent fanciful interpolations thrust into the system by unscrupulous or superstitious people of later times. We would also be in a position to modify them properly to suit modern conditions.

Sometime in the Autumn 1985, Mr. Charles Harvey, whom I met in London, the then President of the Astrological Association of Great Britain suggested that I should give a lecture for an hour during the Annual Function of the Association at Loughborough. I suggested three topics of which, Hindu Synastry was the one selected for my lecture. After the lecture I found that many were interested to know the actual details of the techniques of Hindu Synastry which I naturally could not cover in a brief lecture. It was then that the idea to write a book on Hindu Synastry was born. However, the work of writing the book had to wait for several years as I was always travelling giving seminars and had no time to sit down for the job. Around 1990 a rough version was got ready and translated into French by HIMABINDU, my disciple, to be given as notes to some of my students in France who were interested in the subject.

In writing this book on an astrological subject, I humbly submit I have tried to blaze a new trail. The practice hitherto appears to have been, with a few apologetic exceptions, to quote the Sanskrit verses from the classics, give the translation verbatim and then the explanation with absolutely no independent personal thought contribution or analysis or logical reasoning to support or repudiate what has been said. At best sometimes in the name of critical analysis or comment an attempt is made to pit the dictum of one sage against another and make confusion worse confounded.

I have tried to present the subject in a systematic form with well-defined rules, clear and unambiguous with complete explanations and an analytical commentary. The approach is modern and the style lucid for anyone to learn the technique.

It is my intention to present all aspects of the subject in a proper systematic way with a critical approach. I have often stated my own opinions in the course of the discussions. This does not represent unbridled arrogance or an unabashed attempt to elevate myself in the process of commenting upon the dictums of the sages. Some of my contemporaries or compatriots, in their extreme reverence for the sages may feel so. Far from it, in all humility I submit that it is my own approach to the subject. It is my strong conviction that the lack of a critical approach and in depth study of the theories given by the sages is a great disservice to these intuitive and intellectual giants. It is also my strong conviction that the sages never intended blind faith and acceptance of whatever they said. No true scientist would ever demand such a following and the sages who evolved astrological rules were the greatest scientific thinkers.

My close friend Madame Brigitte FRACHEBOUD, a successful professional Astrologer in Geneva, organized a seminar on

'The philosophy of love and marriage' in the summer of 1994. It was an unusual subject for a Vedic Astrologer to give to Swiss students. As always, my seminar was given extempore. But she was careful and took notes. When this book, which was originally meant to be a guide-book for my students of astrology in Europe, had to be got ready for regular publication, she obliged me with those notes. I am thankful to her. I have included some of that material in the researched article *'The Philosophy of love and marriage.'*

I realize that many readers may not be professional astrologers and may not even know the basics of astrology. For those readers I have prepared a brief mechanical procedure that can be followed with a minimum of understanding of planets and signs to arrive at the right conclusions. Obviously they will have to skip over most of the chapters meant for those initiated in the subject of astrology.

The technique evolved can also be used to study the level of harmony between friends, business associates or teacher and disciple, employer and employee. I have included the necessary modifications to the basic technique to make it applicable for this study.

Vedic astrology is a universal system. It is not related to any religion or faith. It is applicable to all people of all nations. Though India is the land of the Vedas, Vedic wisdom is human heritage.

London
10 February 1999.

K. Jaya Sekhar

The Science, Psychology and Philosophy of Love and Marriage

A MODERN APPROACH

In the modern social set-up clubs, discos, college campuses, holiday resorts and pubs seem to be some of the potential locations to trace the prospective partner. Large number of 'Introduction' agencies are flourishing. Computers have taken over the job that once parents were doing.

'If you want to meet the partner of your dreams' screams an advertisement in an English magazine, 'why not take part in our new national campaign.' Then the advertisement gives *FREE* computer test '*to find your perfect (?) partner*'. The questions to be answered include not only personal details such as age, height, weight, build, color, looks, marital status and religion, but also about occupation, schooling, personality, personal interests and the type of partner one would like. The computer would then pick up the right ones from the pool. That was precisely what the parents were doing when they had the responsibility. It is possible they lost their jobs to the computers when they became more subjective and self-seeking! Then comes the offer in the advertisement, 'All you need is *LOVE'* a paperback to enlighten, of course for a small charge. *All we need is indeed love*!

That is the simple clue to matrimonial joy and happiness. In spite of absolute freedom in matters of sexual relations, freedom to fall in love and choose one's own partner, in many countries, a compatible partner seems to be an elusive proposition. Why are almost forty percent of marriages contracted out of *love* ending up in divorce, sometimes after a bitterly fought legal battle full of acrimonious accusations and use of choice epithets on the 'once upon a time' loved one?

LOVE is the magic word in relationships. We swear by love as the key to the doorway of marital happiness. You first have to *fall in love*. Then starts a courting period and only then comes marriage. How can one marry someone without first falling in love? Love is the prerequisite of marriage. What we are talking about here is *romantic love*. It is the *nurtured love*. It is nurtured today by the stuff we read in novels and teenage magazines, see in movies and TV serials. It is the binding factor in marriage or is it?

THE PSYCHOLOGICAL FORMAT

In 'Introductory Lectures' (1920) Freud tells of three punches that knocked out human pride. First was the discovery by Copernicus that earth, inhabited by humans made in the image of God, was not the center of the universe but only a satellite of the sun. Then came Charles Darwin's theory that we were also members of the animal kingdom having descended from the apes. The third was the theory put forward by Freud himself that our conscious motives and actions (free will) were indeed at the mercy of the uncontrollable forces of the unconsciousness.

Self-preservation and reproduction are the basic instincts of life. *Id* represents these basic instincts. We are born with some basic instincts and carry these into our adulthood. The energy behind these instincts, which is called *Libido,* leads to love in its Sexual and Platonic forms. It constantly fights against hate and hostility. However, it is susceptible to distortions, perversions, obstructions and fixations at any stage of life. Parenting and socializing reign in this energy. Otherwise *Id* would expose clearly our animal instincts. We therefore develop a sense of restraint created by our conscience. This is called *Superego.* 'I', the Ego stands in between instinctive animal drives and the moderating *Superego* created by the external world, continuously performing a balancing act but sometimes slipping one side or the other. *Romantic Love* is one such balancing act. It gives ample opportunity to the Libido without offending the Superego. That is why *falling in love* is so important for all of us. Marriage is only a secondary consequence.

To love, to be in love and to have a companion in love is the most important thing. We have to make a choice as to whom to love. Often it is love at first sight. Sometimes it is love at the second, the third, the fourth or the nth sight. But we do fall in love with someone. *The million dollar question is 'why this one?'*

Sigmund Freud says love is just blocked or delayed sex urge. Havelock Ellis calls it sex-plus-friendship. The psychologist Dorothy Temnov in her book *Love and Limerence* prefers to call it Limerence. Some psychiatrists call it simply- attraction. Helen Fisher a research associate in the Department of Anthropology at the American Museum of Natural History dismisses the whole thing as just–infatuation. It is not important what it is called but what is important is that there is a cluster of characteristics common to all those *deeply in love.*

Love is like all other emotions, a conditional reaction to a situation based on the structure of the superego. But it is a terrible emotional state when you fall in love. There is euphoria in the presence of your beloved and torment in the absence. Dreams continue even while awake. You become absent minded, forgetful. You are writing letters, making phone calls, fixing rendezvous. It is endless prattle, confessions, exaggerations and passionate lovemaking. The world around does not exist and if it does it is meant to be there only for both of you.

Every one entering teenage nurtures a concept of the ideal person with whom they would like to fall in love. Tucked in the pillow of every teenager's bed is this subtle personality that lightens the heart during those early morning misty dreams. Several psychological factors, social inputs including parenting and childhood experiences contribute to this portrait.

Situation is another factor. Psychologists tell us that the emotion of fear can trigger love. Two young people watching a frightening movie or going through a frightening experience could soon find themselves deeply in love.

Then there is the factor of *time.* One is ready to fall in love. And then it *happens.* Scientists have even linked the state of euphoria of being in love to an amine molecule that causes excitement called PEA. However, this state does not seem to be long lasting and the infatuation seems to fade away unless there is the thrill of constant pursuit. Once this thrill of pursuit ends and possession takes place the fading starts.

Love is a game we humans play. Individual nature and nurture decide the way we like to play our games

THE GENETIC FORMAT

We humans are one among the four thousand odd mammals that exist on the face of this earth. Anthropologists estimate that our ancestors evolved only about seven million years ago from the same ancestors of the Chimpanzees. During this period there has been a lot of divergence, though gradual, from the original human form. Genetics tells us that we humans differ from our nearest relatives the African Chimpanzees by only about 1.6% in our nuclear genetic material known as DNA. Sexuality is one aspect, which made our ancestors and the ancestors of Chimpanzees differ. Probably the most significant of the differences are our straight backs and larger brains. That small change makes a large difference in behavior.

Just as anatomy evolves by the process of natural selection so does behavior. The most suitable anatomy and the most favorable behavior that ensures survival and growth naturally get established. Members of the species having such anatomy and behavior are the fittest to survive. We could probably say conversely that we would survive as a species as long as we have that anatomy and that behavior.

Behavior related to sexuality is the male and the female copulating to produce offspring for the survival and growth of the species. The female has a fertile period, known as estrus, when the ova is released and is ready to be fertilized by the sperm. This is known as the period of ovulation. Generally, the female is receptive to copulation during this period. In most animals there are visible signs of this ovulation period. For example in baboons the vagina swells and the skin develops a bright red color advertising the ovulation to the male. Generally, female animals know their fertile period and invite the male through certain sounds or gestures to express their willingness to copulate. The male usually waits for these signals and responds accordingly. Sometimes there is need to compete with, fight and vanquish another male trying to respond to the same female. A behavior pattern is thus established based on this aspect of sexuality. Some females probably copulated with more than one male just as the male was willing to copulate with more than one female in estrus. We call such behavior promiscuous.

It is obvious somewhere along the line of evolution evolved the behavior, where one male copulated with a group of females, a pattern we term as a 'harem'. By the time the Chimps, Gorillas and the Humans evolved as distinct forms of species, different patterns of behavior developed. The Chimps continued to be promiscuous, the Gorillas preferred the harem arrangement and the Humans generally chose monogamy, without abandoning the arrangement of a harem at times. From promiscuity to monogamy is a far cry. However, monogamy is not the monopoly of the human beings. Some animals and birds also follow the system. So also harem and promiscuous behavior are not restricted to other mammals but exist in human sexual behavior as well.

EXCEPTIONAL HUMAN QUALITIES

It is interesting to note that indeed there are some qualities exceptional to the humans. While signs of ovulation are very open and recognizable in most animals it is concealed in the humans and even the female is not aware of her ovulation. Secondly consequent to or for other reasons also sexual receptivity is not limited to the ovulation period. Both male and female do not look forward to a specific period of copulation. Thirdly sex is not indulged in only for procreation but for the mere pleasure of it.

In other words humans indulge in sex as a recreational activity on account of the pleasure it gives. But again recreational sex activity is not an exclusive behavior of the human being. Some animals also seem to be deriving great pleasure out of sex. If duration of the act is any measure of the pleasure derived by the participants, Marsupial mice seem to be getting the most pleasure taking into consideration the twelve hour duration of their copulation! (The evolution of human sexuality by Jared Diamond)

By and large, animals wait for the period of ovulation of the female when only there is receptivity and then indulge in sex for procreation only. Thus the approach is miserly whereas the humans adopt a spendthrift approach.

The distinguishing characteristics of the human beings are thus the unrecognizable period of ovulation, ever-present sexual receptivity and partaking in sex as a source of pleasure. These features have led to certain gender attitudes, certain social behavior and some social problems as well.

ORIGINS OF SOCIAL MONOGAMY

In some animals and birds it is the female alone or the male alone that takes up the responsibility of nurturing the offspring. In some there is a dual parent approach. In the humans there is this dual principle as both father and mother share the responsibility of bringing up the young one. The male, the female and their offspring constitute a unit. Human colonies consist of several such units called 'family'.

The desire of the female is to fertilize her egg with the best possible sperm. But when the exact period of ovulation is not known and there are multiple sexual relationships how would she know whose sperm caused fertilization. The best solution would be to restrict sexual activity to one man. That could easily help pin down the perpetrator. Then to fulfil the combined responsibility to the offspring they live together. Thus monogamy became a necessary aspect of human sexual behavior, an offshoot of the concealed ovulation.

With a high level of Consciousness that we possess as human beings compared to other primates we try to be more organized in our social life. Monogamy became part of this organized social life, an accepted norm of sexual behavior. Religious injunctions, social traditions and civil laws enforced this social behavior.

It is important to realize that social monogamy and genetic monogamy are two entirely different things. In Genetic monogamy there is a built in evolutionary structure ensuring monogamy such as for example in the Marmosal and Tamarin monkeys. They are monogamous by natural instinct. But what about human beings? There seems to be no evidence to suggest that humans are genetically monogamous.

"True monogamy actually is rare," says Stephen T.Emlem, an expert on evolutionary behavior at Cornell University. He adds "There is a great difference between *social monogamy*, where mating pairs bond and work together to raise their young and *genetic monogamy* where parents are faithful sex partners. Social monogamy is relatively common, but genetic monogamy is the exception rather than the rule, the studies report." (From an article by Paul Recer quoting from the journal Science published in The Asian Age, London 26-09-1998.)

Social monogamy suited the human beings. Basically it solved the problem for the female with unrecognizable period of ovulation to know who had sired her child. Secondly with constant receptivity to sex she ensured the man never strayed in search of sex. It was also necessary for the female to be faithful to her man. Conceiving to another could bring catastrophic consequences. Since ovulation was concealed, unfaithfulness was too risky an adventure for the female. Social monogamy was a necessary sexual behavior.

THE INSTITUTION OF MARRIAGE

In an organized and civilized society there was the need to socially recognize which pair constituted a parent unit responsible for the care of the children and who had to be faithful to whom. Thus came into existence the social institution called *Marriage.* Basically it is a process by which society recognizes the commitment of a man and woman to sexual fidelity for a lifetime. Under those circumstances the identity of the progeny is well-established. Not only maternity but also paternity is then a certainty.

Religious commandments, moral and civil codes centered round social monogamy in the form of marriage as the most cherished social value in life. Mutual faithfulness as a mandatory condition of male-female relationship was extolled through several stories, parables in mythology and religious books. Several societies condemned unfaithfulness in marriage. Some made it a crime attracting capital punishment.

GENETIC AND SOCIAL CONFLICT

The genetic structure makes the female seek sperms of a male of a 'high' quality (intellectually, physically, or materially) so she could produce offspring that will survive better and withstand competition for existence. The genetic structure of the male is to impregnate as many as possible to ensure the survival of the species. These structures do not call for monogamy.

Gowarty, a behavioral ecologist at the University of Georgia, reports that of 180 socially monogamous species he studied, only about ten percent were sexually faithful and human beings were not in that ten percent!

There seems to be a paradoxical situation. Social monogamy is a natural consequence of evolution but at the same time it conflicts with evolved gene-prompted behavior.

Marriage ensures social monogamy but it is contradictory to genetic needs. The farmer (male) is in constant search of fertile fields (females) to sow as many wild oats as possible to increase the tribe. The fertile fields (females) are always waiting for the farmer (male) with the finest oats so that they could yield produce of exceptional quality, survival being the essential aim of genetic evolution.

A SOLUTION : AN ESCAPE ROUTE

Monogamy and sexual fidelity ensured through the institution of marriage in human societies stifled genetic behavior. Soon an escape route was found in the form of *divorce.* On one ground or the other the couple could separate. This ensured the identity of the offspring, provided combined care and attention and also provided the opportunity for gene-prompted behavior through remarriage. A couple could go through any number of *divorce-remarriage* experiences as a compromise solution. Social scientists call it serial monogamy. The disparaging term promiscuous can be avoided. Men and women are faithful to their *current* partners.

In spite of religion frowning upon humans trying to cast as under those joined together in 'sacred' matrimony, divorce has come to stay as a social process as much as marriage. The rate of divorce is reaching 50 percent level in most of the advanced countries. Developing countries are also trying to catch up on this social level apart from the economic level.

BUT ALL IS NOT WELL

Gene dictated behavior restricted sometimes in very inhuman ways, through religious injunctions and social laws tried to assert itself through a major revolution popularly known as the feminist movement in the mid sixties. As a by-product of that revolution came a major sexual revolution. Feminists fought for equal rights with men and for what they called absolute right over their own bodies. This obviously implied and included the right to have sex with whom they wanted, when they wanted. They could also refuse to copulate with the wedded husband if they so chose. Most of the Governments responded with appropriate laws that gave these rights to women. I am not for a moment suggesting that sexual liberty bordering on licentiousness is the result of the feminist movement. That movement did give an opportunity for gene inspired behavior to assert itself over socially contrived behavior. The movement and the consequences could be a conspiracy of the Universe itself to usher in some evolutionary processes.

With divorce and serial monogamy well in place in society, this new found liberty gave woman the opportunity to seek copulation without reference or relation to ovulation with whomsoever they desired and considered the best. It suited the men also who were as much anxious to sow wherever possiblc. Premarital relations, extramarital relations, promiscuous relations, male and female sexual harassment became common.place in society. Some are inclined to attribute the sexual revolution to the advent of the 'Pill'.

Whatever prompted the revolution, the result was that the institution of marriage itself collapsed much to the delight of the Selfish Gene. (Book tittle of the famous British Biologist Richard Dawking).

Sex without commitment is the name of the game and the winner is – THE GENE.

UNCOMFORTABLE STATISTICS

Now that the male was no longer the only provider and certainly could not play the role of 'head of the family' dictating to the rest, it suited both the male and female to form an undefined relationship, euphemistically called 'living together'. This meant there was no commitment on either side in any way. For the woman it was a symbol of her emancipation, a state of freedom and liberty. For the man it meant there was no obligation to any religious vows or social laws. When 'love' became a past tense, the cumbersome legal process of divorce was no longer necessary.

"New York: A growing body of research has found that people who live together before marriage are more likely than other couples to divorce."

"According to a report released this week from the US National Marriage Project at Rutgers University, studies done over the past decade found the same connection between living together before marriage and splitting up after. Many researchers believe the reason is partly that people who live together are more unconventional to begin with and are less committed to the institution of marriage and more open to the possibility of divorce.

The authors of the latest report suspect something more insidious, that living together slowly *erodes people's ability to commit* (Emphasis mine) and their faith in the institution of marriage." (An AP news release in The Asian Age, London, dated 4-2-99)

The human male goes on impregnating with impunity and without responsibility. The human female motivated by the desire to get the best, cheated by her concealed ovulation, notwithstanding the Pill being her best friend, ends up with the care of the offspring *alone*.

Let us see the scores of this *game* in the U.K. for example, 1.5-m lone parents care for 2-m children. 57 percent are divorced, widowed or separated women, 33 percent are women who never married and only 9 percent are men. Out of 43 percent who have an agreement for maintenance only 33 percent receive the amount. (Statistics published by Yvoune Roberts in the SUNDAY TIMES Magazine in her article 'The truth about single mothers')

The Universe endowed the human being with the highest level of consciousness. Consciousness is awareness and awareness of oneself means a clear concept of identity. The first level of identity for a human being is the parental unit. Children whose parental identity was unclear because they were born out of promiscuous, pre-marital or extra-marital sex and children whose parental unit had broken, lost their own sense of identity, self esteem and purpose in life and most often became anti-social in their attitudes and activities.

Let us see what these Lost Children have been doing in the country referred as *The Greatest Nation*- the U.S.A. "At a meeting of the Homicide Research Working Group, a nation wide alliance of academic and government researchers, Alfred Blumstein of Carnegie Mellon University argued that the rise of homicides by boys under 18 began in 1985, following 15 years of flat lines". (Special report published in the NEWS WEEK, August 15, 1994)

"From about 8 offences per 100,000 committed by boys between 14 and 17 in 1975 the figure doubles to 17 by 1990 with an upward trend starting from 1985." (Source: James A.Fox, Glenn Pierce, and National Crime Analysis program, NORTH-EASTERN UNIV.)

Certainly these children born around 1970, probably under the gene prompted sexual behavior of their parents, had lost their sense of human values and so had no regard for human life. However it is important to realize that parental separation alone may not be the sole cause for juvenile criminality. There could be other reasons, which could be the main or contributing factors.

AN ABIDING SOLUTION IN VEDIC SOCIETY

A technologist modifies and improves his products learning from experience. Each new generation is a better product. The Universe also evolves better genetic codes. Millions of years of attempts to evolve the fittest and ablest helped create the genetic code of the human being. The fascinating part in this code is the one related to the brain and the sensory system. It makes the human being an outstanding product capable of attempting to control and conquer Nature. Man has succeeded in this attempt to some extent. That there is a backlash from Nature is a different story.

On account of a more powerful mental capacity and a high level of discrimination man can understand, analyze, control or moderate genetic behavior. Through proper *nurture and conditioning* this (changing the selfish gene to a social gene) can be achieved. Man has the means for better discrimination in choosing and evolving a constructive social behavior. Unlike certain mammals whose behavior is within the framework of the genetic code, man has the means to choose. He can evolve a behavior that synthesizes genetic sexual compulsions and the requirements of a civilized society.

The civilization developed on the banks of the rivers Sindhu and Saraswati in north India, popularly known as the Vedic civilization effectively created this synthesis. Though many mammals have some kind of group organization, civilization is a special feature of human society. Two great thinkers of the twentieth century defined civilization in their own way. Sigmund Freud in his essay (1915) 'Thoughts for the Times of War and Death' says "civilization has been attained through the renunciation of instincts". His Holiness the Dalai Lama has defined civilization as "the recognition of certain values in life." Human society, to be considered civilized, has to recognize certain values of life and try to respect those values by restricting and renouncing instinctual behavior contrary to those values. These values have to be established on the basis of the welfare of the human species as a whole without totally abandoning individual freedom, peace and happiness. *The Selfish Gene has to reform itself into a Social gene.*

SANSKARAS

With this objective the learned ancient habitants on the plains of Sindhu and Saraswati rivers in the north of India, evolved a comprehensive, liberal social structure. It has been well described in the writings of sages. The most interesting aspect of this structure is the *Sanskaras*. The literal meaning of the word *Sanskara* is 'to reform'. What is to be reformed? It is the gene-prompted behavior in the human being. These *Sanskaras* strengthen the brainpower, the mental faculties, the power of discrimination, the level of consciousness, so that the person going through these *Sanskaras* becomes a refined person.

They have indicated sixteen such *Sanskaras* to be performed in the life of an individual at certain ages starting from birth. One who goes through these enlightening rituals is capable of developing a very constructive social behavior. Where everyone in a society goes through these *Sanskaras*, there is evidence of a social behavior that ensures happiness, contentment and peaceful existence.

VIVAHA SANSKARA

One of these SANSKARAS is known as VIVAHA, the marriage ritual. The Vivaha Sanskara involves the performance of certain rituals. (1) The bride and groom are ritualistically prepared for the marriage. (2) The parents offer their children in marriage. (3) The couple makes their promises in front of the Sacrificial Fire lit for the purpose and also to the Elements. (4) The groom places a thread with a pendant or a chain in the neck of the bride and the bride places a ring on the finger of the groom. (5) The couple make perambulations around the Sacrificial Fire and take seven steps together, symbolically indicating willingness to live together through thick and thin. There is a profound impact at the sub conscious and conscious levels by the ritual. The priest explains the rights and responsibilities as husband and wife and also what society expects of them. The recitation of the relevant Mantras (chants) and the symbolical actions which the bride and groom perform during the ceremony have a hypnotic effect. It is a reforming and enlightening procedure. This SANSKARA is responsible for the refinement of nature and the nurture of certain values in life.

However as population increases, congested towns and cities come into existence, complications and tensions develop in society. It becomes difficult to enforce a uniform pattern of marriage for all. In the *Smriti* literature we find that ancient society, better named the Vedic Society recognized and accepted eight kinds of marriages.

1. BRAHMA VIVAHA: A marriage arranged by the parents of the bride and groom with their consent and performed with Vedic rituals.
2. DAIVA VIVAHA: This is marriage-between a boy and girl who belong to the priestly community, those who perform rituals and religious ceremonies especially in temples.
3. ARSHA VIVAHA: Gifts are taken from the groom and given to the bride as a part of the marriage ceremony. (Obviously performed by those belonging to the economically higher strata)
4. PRAJAPATYA VIVAHA: A promise is extracted from the groom that he would take all responsibilities of a husband and as the head of the family and never renounce such duties in favor of another style of life.
5. RAKSHASA VIVAHA: When a man kidnaps a woman, the kidnapper is obliged to marry her and take up the responsibility of looking after her.

6. ASURA VIVAHA: When a young man has a strong desire to marry a certain girl, he may offer money and or gifts to the girl and the girl's parents to induce them to agree for the marriage and then get married with proper rituals.
7. GANDHARVA VIVAHA: A marriage resulting out of mutual love. When a boy and girl fall in love and desire to get married they simply garland one another. They are then considered as husband and wife. They may do so in a temple or before some responsible witnesses. Subsequently if they so desire they may go through the regular marriage ritual.
8. PAISHACHIKA VIVAHA: When a man rapes a woman, he is obliged to marry her and take all responsibility.

When we study the procedures of the marriages recognized we feel that it was the woman who was a scarce commodity and men had to often give gifts to secure a wife. The position seemed to have reversed itself either because of demographic changes or certain political conditions that came into existence consequent to the land of Aryans being invaded by several foreign cultures. It became the custom for the girl's parents to pay a heavy price to secure a groom.

Mutual love leading to marriage is not an invention of modern society. It existed even in the days of Vedic civilization and society accepted such a marriage even though probably either or both the parents disapproved of it. Indian mythology has many such instances. In those days, characters in mythologies and epics inspired *romantic love.*

The million dollar question 'why this one?' was answered in a different way. In the first four categories the marriage may be considered as arranged marriage. The parents of the boy and girl are very much involved in the process. The usual procedure is for the parents of the boy and the girl to first secure the horoscopes and get them compared by a competent astrologer for compatibility. This takes care of the philosophical, karmic and subtle energy aspects of the prospective couple. Once the astrologer selects a few charts reasonably compatible then the parents get to know each other. On the practical side they check up all factors such as age, appearances, family background, education, health, aptitudes, family culture, social culture, economic situation and expectations and ambitions in life. Generally, one or more of these factors are responsible for the break up of the marriage. They ensure that no conflict can arise in these areas. Then the boy and girl are introduced to one another so that they can give their approval. The information collected by the parents is certainly passed on to the young ones. The entire information is known to the prospective partners to enable them to come to a decision. If one of them disapproves of the other, the marriage does not take place. This is generally the procedure, even today in India, at least in the middle class families that follow traditions.

CONDITIONING RULES

Dr. R.B.Pandey in his scholarly work, *HINDU SANSKARAS* (*Motilal Banarsidass. Delhi 1987*) says, "There is no instance of promiscuity proper in Vedic Literature. The only reference to it is found in the *MAHABHARATA*. There it is stated that women were free in early primitive times and they could have sexual relations with anybody they liked, even though they were married. *Swetaketu*, son of Uddalaka, however, abolished this custom. This story, at most proves that the Aryans had passed through a stage of society when such intercourse was tolerated in society."

Smritis and *Sutras*, part of Vedic Literature, describe in detail the procedure for the *VIVAHA SANSKARA*. At this point I would like to mention that one of the rules is that a boy and girl belonging to the same *GOTRA* should not be married. In ancient times children of a family, brothers and sisters studied in the Ashram of one sage and followed his teachings. For instance if they were the disciples of the *GURU KOUNDINYA*, they considered themselves to belong to *KOUNDINYASA GOTRA*. Those who had the same *GURU* obviously were related as brothers and sisters or their progeny. The object of the rule is to avoid such close marriages.

However, they also state that the parental relationship should be traced backwards only for seven generations and beyond that the concept of 'same origin' ceases. Besides genetic diseases in the family was also investigated for seven generations to avoid marriages leading to genetically malformed handicapped children. Apparently it looks like some superstitious numerology adapted for convenience. Does it make any scientific sense?

We are aware that 23 chromosomes of the father and 23 chromosomes of the mother combine to form the cell of the human embryo. The defects of the father or the mother are thus passed on to the progeny. If one of the parents has a defect, since half of the chromosomes go to the child, there is a 50 percent chance of the child developing that defect. Thus there is a .5 percent chance in the first generation, .255 in the second, .125 percent in the third, .0625 percent in the fourth, .03125 percent in the fifth, .015625 percent in the sixth, .0078125 percent in the seventh and .00390625 percent in the eighth generation. This figure indicates that in the eighth generation, out of 100,000 children born to Gotra related couples, only 3 may be born with the defect, a negligibly small number. That gives some scientific sense to the rule.

The essence of the system seems to be:

1. To define a legitimate sexual relationship,
2. To ensure monogamy,
3. To ensure parental identity to the children,
4. To ensure security of a home for the children,
5. To ensure physically healthy, mentally strong and psychologically secure growth of children, who can become useful and constructive members of an integrated and well-organized society, and
6. To ensure a society which recognizes, accepts and follows certain social values.

It should also be stated that divorce and separation were not absolutely prohibited. Where the marriage was found to be a total failure and the couple living together harmed themselves, the children and effected the peace and harmony of the society, separation was recommended.

The institution of marriage was an important aspect of regulated *VEDIC Society*. It was considered a welcome stage of life, eagerly awaited both by men and women. Marriage was a 'commitment.' Both the partners knowingly, willingly and honestly took up that 'commitment.' Love was a future tense word in the traditional marriage. Marriage marked the beginning of the process of developing deep love, a love that transcended the levels of romantic idealism, of physical ecstasy and reached the glorious levels of the union of souls.

"There are three levels in the relationship between man and woman. The first is *Akarshana* (attraction). At first sight there is the physical appeal, the appeal of the personality. This is the primary requirement. Then after they get to 'know' each other, they develop mental harmony, mutual understanding, deep love and consideration for each other. They realize how complimentary there are to each other. They develop *Anuraga* (mutual love & metal harmony). These two levels are necessary for the 'commitment' in marriage to be fulfilled. Only when these two levels exist there can be fruitful 'commitment.' It assures a long married life of happiness and contentment with mentally and emotionally well-balanced children. Such a long marital life leads to *Anubandha* (eternal bond). There is then a harmony at the level of the *Atmas.* The desire to live together as one gets so deep rooted that they wish to be couples life after life. Such *Anubandha* pre-pares one for and ensures marital success even in the life after. Kindred *Atmas* recognize and realize their karmic togetherness coming from past life." (From my book BED OF ROSES-UNDER-STANDING INDIAN HERITAGE.)

Love between a couple is considered an emotional state of mind, a condition brought over through years of making and keeping a home together. The husband and wife bring forth children and love them as part of their own bodies. They partake of all the responsibilities that go with bringing up children and making them mature adults and responsible citizens. They also enjoy the pleasure of seeing the young ones grow from helpless infancy to the exploring childhood, from experimenting teens to ambitious adolescence, from the unsure adult to the confident individual. They share the responsibility of finding the material resources to maintain the family, the work involved in feeding, clothing, caring, healing and entertaining a family. They face the joys and sufferings, the dark days and the sunny days together. It is through that, giving, receiving and sharing; each recognizes the need and value of the other, the importance of the other in his or her life. In due course they come to feel 'I am you and you are me. I do not exist without you, nor you without me.' That unified feeling, a unity at the level of the Inner Self, is the state of LOVE that was aimed at in the 'Vedic Vivaha Sanskara.' "Only love of a spiritual nature is abiding. Such love is made of a different stuff".

At the end of the day all that counts is whatever is good for the survival of the human race and whatever makes human life happy and peaceful. With this objective human beings have to be parented, nurtured and socialized. Children need the care and attention of both the parents as much as they need the identity established by the parent unit. It gives them a sense of security, self esteem, a sense of belonging and a purpose in life. Such a generation can be bred only if there are more and more loving couples and long lasting marriages. A broken marriage is not only damaging to the psyche of the children but also traumatic experience for the couple. Though some couples get happily remarried broken marriages often create frustrated men and women and the experience of a failed marriage makes them less confident, more hesitant and suspicious. *Once bitten twice shy.* There are fewer chances of subsequent relationships lasting long. There is a saying "To err is human but only fools re-marry". The implication is that one is no wiser a second time! But nothing prevents one from *becoming* wiser and therefore happy and successful the second time.

"After spending 11 years analyzing thousands of questionnaires, Oxford professor Michael Argyle believes he has found out what makes people happy. Prof. Argyle told the *Sunday Telegraph* newspaper that the key was to have one close relationship and a network of friends. Marriage was one of the most important guarantees of happiness, especially for men and the least happy in society were those who are divorced or separate, his research found." (Asian Age, London D.4-10-98)

If as His Holiness the Dalai Lama defined, civilization is the recognition of certain values of life, desiring a happy sustaining married life is one cherished value.

Introduction

In writing this book on an astrological subject, I humbly submit I have tried to blaze a new trail. The practice hitherto appears to have been, with a few apologetic exceptions, to quote the Sanskrit verses from the classics, give the translation verbatim and then the explanation with absolutely no independent personal thought contribution or analysis or logical reasoning to support or repudiate what has been said. At times the author pits the dictum of one sage against another and makes confusion worse confounded. I have tried to present the subject in a systematic form with well-defined rules, clear and unambiguous with complete explanations and an analytical commentary. The approach is modern and the style lucid for anyone to learn the technique.

It is my intention to present all aspects of the subject in a proper systematic way with a critical approach. I have often stated my own opinions in the course of the discussions. This does not represent unbridled arrogance or an unabashed attempt to elevate myself in the process of commenting upon the dictums of the Sages. Some of my contemporaries or compatriots, in their extreme reverence for the sages may feel so. Far from it, in all humility I submit that it is my own approach to the subject. It is my strong conviction that the lack of a critical approach and an in depth study of the theories given by sages is a great disservice to these intuitive and intellectual giants. It is also my strong conviction that the sages never intended blind faith and acceptance of whatever they said. No true scientist would ever demand such a following and the Sages who evolved Astrological rules were the greatest scientific thinkers.

I realize that many readers may not be professional astrologers and may not even know the basics of astrology. For those readers I have prepared a brief mechanical procedure that can be followed with a minimum of understanding of planets and signs to arrive at the right conclusions. Obviously they will have to skip over most of the chapters meant for those initiated in the subject of Vedic Astrology.

The technique evolved can also be used to study the level of harmony between friends, business associates or teacher and disciple, employer and employee. I have included the necessary modifications to the basic technique to make it applicable for this study.

To break the shackles of traditional puritanism in astrology books, while using Sanskrit names for planets and signs, I have often used the English names as well. Understanding the correlation of planetary configurations to evolving human life is not related to language and literature but to philosophical inquiry and scientific technic.

Many books written by sociologists, psychologists and counselors explain how to make the right choice; develop proper communication with the partner, and how to keep the relationship going. They are based on experience, experiments and statistical data collected by various organizations studying human relationships. They critically analyze the causes for marital unhappiness and breakdown of relationships. They present tried and proved methods for success.

This book is based on Vedic Astrology, a statistical science that correlates planetary configurations with human emotions, motivations and life experiences. It is based on the Vedic astrological method of comparing birth charts for marriage. It aims at the same objective of ensuring a successful, happy and long relationship but employs a different technique.

Those for whom companionship is just another form of entertainment, there are many sun-sign astrological fun books. But this book is meant for people who consider marriage a social commitment, who take relationships seriously and for whom companionship is not just fun but is something that inspires, transforms and satisfies the deep urge to love and be loved and has a deeper divine meaning and purpose.

The meeting of two personalities is like
The contact of two chemical substances.
If there is any reaction,
Both are transformed. —Carl Jung

This book tries to help you to astrologically identify *the two chemically reacting personalities.* That's THE BEST BET for transformation and sustaining satisfaction in a relationship.

PART I

VEDIC ASTROLOGY : BASICS

CHAPTER 1

Quick Start Method

If you do not have a fairly good knowledge of astrology and do not desire to go further than learning a few fundamentals of astrology you can still use this book, though in a mechanical way.

The broad path along which the planets orbit in space is called the Zodiac. It is an elliptical path of 360 degrees. It is divided into twelve parts of 30 degrees each. Each part is called a Zodiac Sign. They can be identified in the skies with the help of the constellations in them.

The twelve signs in the Zodiac are: *Aries, Taurus, Gemini, Cancer, Leo, Virgo, Libra, Scorpio, Sagittarius, Capricorn, Aquarius* and *Pisces* in that order. In the system commonly called the Western system of astrology the Zodiac starts, that is the 0 deg. of Aries is at the point where the apparent path of the Sun cuts the line of the Equator extended in space. This point is known as the Vernal Equinox. In the Vedic System it starts at a fixed star. At a point of time both these starting points coincided and there was no problem. However, the Vernal Equinox keeps moving backwards every year by a small value. After several years this value becomes quite large making the charts made on the basis of the Western System and Vedic System differ by several degrees. This difference is known as the precession of the equinoxes *(Ayanamsa)*.

Only nine planets, *Sun*, *Moon*, *Mars*, *Mercury*, *Jupiter*, *Venus*, *Saturn* and the two nodes called *Rahu* and *Ketu* are used in Vedic astrology. The nodes are really not planetary bodies but only the points where the line of orbit of Moon cuts the line of apparent orbit of the Sun.

A Birth Chart is a diagram showing the twelve Zodiac signs with the planets placed in them at the precise degrees and minutes as they were on the precise date and time of birth. The birth chart also shows which degree of the Zodiac was at the eastern horizon at the precise moment of birth as viewed from the place of birth.

This point of the Zodiac is called the Ascendant. As the earth is rotating on its axis towards the east, this ascendant point keeps continuously moving, with the signs of the Zodiac rising in the east.

There are books called ephemeris, which give the positions of the planets as well as the astronomical information to calculate the ascendant. We now also have computers programmed to give the Birth Charts when you feed in the birth details. For a modest fee you can get your Birth Chart from any source supplying you with Birth Charts. Since the system in this book is based on the Vedic system it is necessary that you secure your Birth Chart made in the Vedic system, which is known as the Siderial system. In case you are able to get only the Birth Chart in the Western system you can very easily convert it into the Siderial system.

All you need to do is take a paper and note down the longitude in degrees and minutes and sign in which each of the nine planets and the ascendant are in your birth chart according to the Western system. Then turn to Page No.14 where you have the Table *AYANAMSA*. It is the value of the difference between the two systems. *Note the Ayanamsa value in degrees and minutes (seconds can be neglected) for the particular year of birth in this Table.* Then *deduct* this value from the degrees and minutes of each of the nine planets and the ascendant which you have noted down. You will get the position of the nine planets and the ascendant in degrees and minutes and the signs in the Siderial system.

Note that when the Ayanamsa degrees you want to deduct is higher than the planet's longitude degrees, you need to add 30 degree to the existing planet's degrees and then deduct. The result is the position of the planet in the *preceding* sign.

For example, a person is born in the year 1956. In the birth chart Venus is in Scorpio 12 deg 22 mts. (12°-22'). In the *AYANAMSA TABLE* we find for the year 1956, the value is 23°15'.

Venus is in Scorpio, that is 8th sign	12°-22'
It is necessary to add one sign =	30°
	42°- 22'
Ayanamsa to be deducted	23°-15'
Venus is in Libra, that is 7th sign	19°-07'

So in the Sidereal Birth Chart you will have to put Venus in Libra at 19°-07'.

SIMPLE PROCEDURE

Simply draw a square like the diagram below in which the Sign positions are always fixed.

Pisces	Aries	Taurus	Gemini
Aquari			Cancer
Capri			Leo
Sagitt	Scorpio	Libra	Virgo

Find the Sidereal positions of all the planets and the ascendant for both the charts to be compared for compatibility. Then place the planets and the ascendant in the corresponding signs as indicated by their longitudes.

EXAMPLE: Person born on 27-8-1932, at 13h 25m G.M.T at a place Lat. 16°-54' North and Long: 81°-09' East. From the table we note for the year 1932, the Ayanamsa is 22°-54' 58". Adjusting to minutes we can take 22°-55'. I give below the Western system longitudes and the Sidereal system longitudes obtained by deducting the Ayanamsa from the Western system longitudes.

Asnd: 12" 14° 58'
22° 55'
11" 22° 03'

Sun: 6" 04° 02'
22° 55'
5" 11° 07'

Moon: 4" 10° 47'
22° 55'
3" 17° 52'

Mars: 4" 14° 51'
22° 55'
3" 21° 56'

Mer: 5" 19° 16'
22° 55'
4" 26° 21'

Jup: 6" 3° 29'
22° 55'
5" 10° 34'

Ven: 4" 18° 41'
22° 55'
3" 25° 46'

Sat: 10" 29° 06'
22° 55'
10" 06° 11'

Rah: 12" 17° 36'
22° 55'
11" 24° 41'

Ketu: 6" 17° 36'
22° 55'
5" 24° 41'

The standard square chart is drawn and the planets are then placed in the corresponding signs showing their longitudes. The Birth Chart with these planetary positions is shown as below:

<table>
<tr><td></td><td></td><td></td><td>Moon 17°-52'
Mars 21°-56'
Ven 25°-46'</td></tr>
<tr><td>Rahu 24°-41'
Asnd 22°-03'</td><td colspan="2" rowspan="2">Birth Chart</td><td>Mer 26°-21'</td></tr>
<tr><td>Sat 06°-11'</td><td>Jup 10°-34'
Sun 11°-07'
Ket 24°-41'</td></tr>
<tr><td></td><td></td><td></td><td></td></tr>
</table>

Once you have learnt to make the Birth Chart, note the longitude of Moon. In the above chart it is 17°-52' Gemini. Now go to Page No. 18 where a table is given. In the table in coloumn 4 under Range we find the range 6°-40' to 20° of Gemini given in column 5. Under column name of Nakshatra (lunar signs) we have the name Ardra whose serial number is 6. It is enough if you note that the Nakshtra of this person is No.6.

Now read on from Chapter 5, THE LOTUS OF SIX PETALS. Omit chapters on petals 4 and 5, which require the full study of *Sandwich course of Vedic Astrology* given in the next chapter. In the final evaluation also you can omit these petals 4 and 5. You will still get a good understanding of the compatibility. The ready reckoner tables at the end of the book will give instant evaluation.

As you get to work on more and more charts, you will develop the necessary interest and knowledge to study and understand the full subject. Do not be diffident because you do not have much back- ground knowledge of Astrology. Get started and you will soon master the technique. Good Luck.

CHAPTER 2

Sandwich Course of Vedic Astrology

This chapter is given for the benefit of those who want to learn the fundamentals of *Vedic Astrology,* so that they can make use of the system explained in this book with a better perception. I should state that this chapter is not meant to be a condensed course on *Hindu Astrology.* Only the basics relevant and required for the use of the systems given in this book are explained in this chapter, in a concise way. No one reading through this chapter should presume that he or she has fully studied Vedic Astrology and certainly should not rush to use this limited knowledge for judging matrimonial and sentimental life of an individual from the horoscope.

PLANETS

In Vedic Astrology NINE planets are used. Their Indian names and universal symbols are as given below :

1.	Sun	☉	SURYA (OR RAVI)
2.	Moon	☽	CHANDRA
3.	Mars	♂	KUJA(or ANGARAKA or MANGAL)
4.	Mercury	☿	BUDHA
5.	Jupiter	♃	GURU (or BRIHASPATI)
6.	Venus	♀	SHUKRA
7.	Saturn	♄	SHANI
8.	North Node	☊	RAHU
9.	South Node	☋	KETU

In the above, the seven planets are given in the order of the week days they rule, starting from Sunday. The last two are really not planets but only 'Points' in space which will be explained later.

In the Solar system the Sun is in the centre with all the planets including our Earth orbiting around it in their fixed orbits. Moon, a satellite of the Earth orbits round the Earth. However, when we observe from the earth, we find the Sun apparently orbiting the Earth. This apparent path of the Sun is known as the ecliptic. This ecliptic is inclined at an angle to the Celestial Equator, which is the extension into space of the earth's equator. Therefore, the Ecliptic and the Celestial equator intersect each other, at two points. These are known as the equinoxes. On March 21st the Sun is at a point on the Ecliptic where it cuts the equator and moves to the North. This point is called the *Vernal Equinox*. Six months later on September 21st it is at the opposite point moving South. This point is called the *Autumnal Equinox*.

We have seen that the Moon has its own orbit round the earth. This orbit of the Moon, naturally intersects the Ecliptic at two points. These points are called the North Node, (Rahu) and South Node, (Ketu). The point where Moon moves to the South of the ecliptic is Ketu, and to the North is Rahu.

THE ZODIAC

Observed from the Earth all the planets move against the starry background. It is also found that the orbits of these planets are not widely far off but limited to a belt. We have already seen that the apparent path of the Sun is the ecliptic. If we take a range of 9 degrees on either side of this ecliptic we find that the orbits of all the planets fall within this belt. This belt is called the *Zodiac*. There are particular star groups or constellations that form the background of this belt. The particular constellations against which the planets appear to move are specially important.

This circular path is 360 degrees. The best way to mark this imaginary path, the Zodiac, is to mark on the basis of the stars which we can see in the background.

The Zodiac is divided into 12 equal parts, called the signs of the Zodiac. The Sun takes one year to travel along the Zodiac. Since the year has twelve months, the Sun takes one month to move through one sign of the Zodiac.

The question is, where do we have the first point of the circular Zodiac, to commence the divisions. The ancients picked up a certain star in the background, and marked off equal parts of 30° from there, making twelve divisions.

The following table gives the twelve signs of the Zodiac with their names in English and Sanskrit, symbols, their planetary rulers and their symbols.

No.	NAMES			RULING	
	ENGLISH	SANSKRIT		PLANET- SYMBOL	
1.	Aries	MESHAM	♈	KUJA	♂
2.	Taurus	VRISHABHAM	♉	SHUKRA	♀
3.	Gemini	MITHUNAM	♊	BUDHA	☿
4.	Cancer	KATAKAM	♋	CHANDRA	☽
5.	Leo	SIMHAM	♌	SURYA	☉
6.	Virgo	KANYA	♍	BUDHA	☿
7.	Libra	TULA	♎	SHUKRA	♀
8.	Scorpio	VRISHCHIKAM	♏	KUJA	♂
9.	Sagittarius	DHANUS	♐	GURU	♃
10.	Capricorn	MAKARA	♑	SHANI	♄
11.	Aquarius	KUMBHA	♒	SHANI	♄
12.	Pisces	MEENA	♓	GURU	♃

You will note that excepting Surya and Chandra the other five planets rule two signs each. Rahu and Ketu are not given any rulers. The Solar System with the planets, the earth, and the Zodiac against the starry background is shown in the following figure.

THE ZODIAC AND THE PLANETS

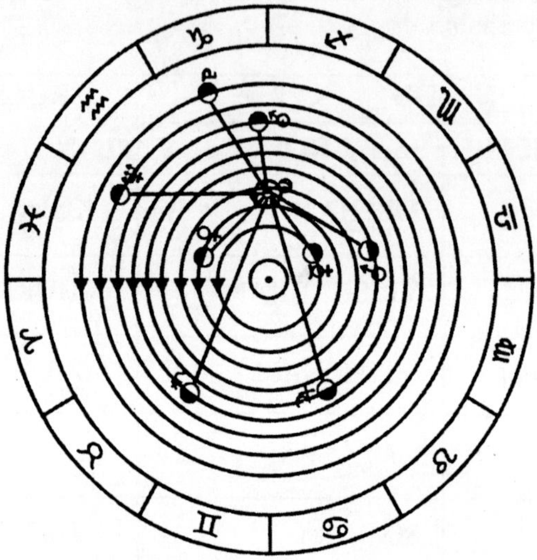

The figure shows the Sun in the centre of the Solar System with the planets marked on their orbits round the Sun. The Moon has its orbit round the Earth. Planets travel along the orbits at fixed individual speeds. You will note the orbits of Venus and Mercury lie between the Sun and the Earth's orbit. We have the background of the Stars. On this background is the Zodiac which is the broad path in which all the orbits of the planets lie. Observed from the Earth, at any instant, the various planets including the Sun appear to be travelling through the various Zodiac signs. This can be seen in the above illustration.

LAGNA (Ascendant)

Because of the Earth's rotation on its axis towards the East, the Zodiac signs appear to rise in the East and set in the West. In a day of 24 hours all the zodiac signs rise and set, as Earth makes one complete rotation round its axis in 24 hours.

At the moment of birth not only do we find the planets at different points in the Zodiac but also, observed from the place of birth on the eastern horizon, we find a certain Zodiac sign rising. The degree of the sign rising on the east is called the Lagna or Ascending Degree.

RASHI CHAKRA (HOROSCOPE CHART)

At the moment of birth, planets are at particular points in the Zodiac. The Chart or Map of Heavens for the moment of birth shows the positions of the Planets and the Ascendent in the Zodiac. Hence the Zodiac of twelve signs are to be drawn. In India we have several forms of the Zodiac drawn. The simplest form used in South India is shown in the following figure. In this chart the positions of the Zodiac signs are fixed. The planets as per their positions, seen in the ephemeris are placed in the Zodiac. The sign rising in the East, that is the Lagna is also calculated and marked in the Zodiac. This chart is known as the Rashi Chart.

For the chart a simple square form is used specially in South India. The position of the signs is always fixed in this diagram. That is Aries is always in the second square on the top row and the signs follow in a clockwise direction. The Ascendent or Lagna and the planets with their longitudes in degrees and minutes are placed in the signs as calculated from the Ephemeris. The signs are not usually marked; only the planets are noted in the squares as the sign positions are always the same.

The fixed sign positions are given in the following figure.

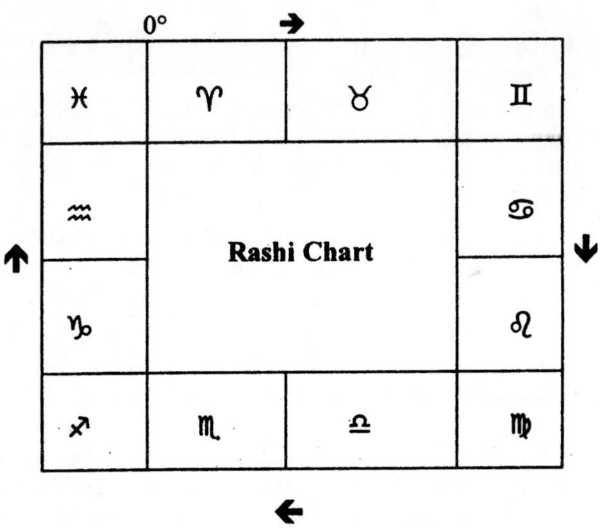

It is important to note that the zodiacal signs are placed clockwise here.

An example of a blank Rashi Chart :

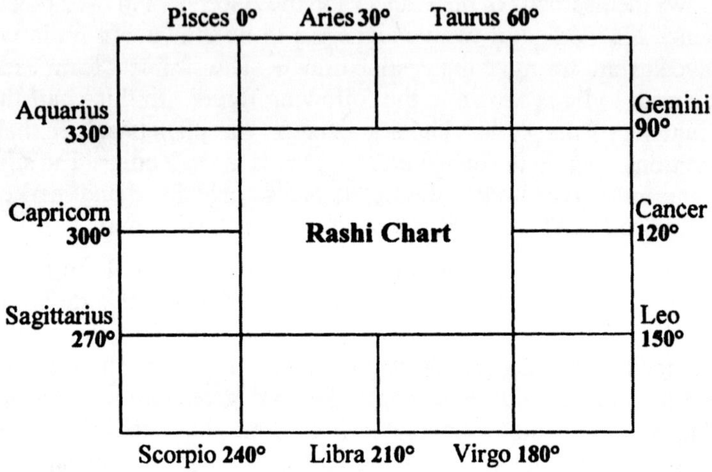

AYANAMSA

In the third Century AD it was thought that the Zodiac divisions should begin at the Vernal Equinox, instead of the fixed star considered by the ancients. Probably around 356 AD the star from which the Zodiac was marked in antiquity and the vernal Equinox coincided. So this difference of marking the start of the Zodiac from the vernal equinox instead of the fixed star did not matter. But much later it was discovered that the Vernal Equinox point kept moving backward along the ecliptic at the rate of about 50 seconds per year. Though this is a very small value, in the course of many years this difference becomes considerable and then it does matter. For example, for the year 1999 it has been worked out that the distance between the Equinox and the fixed star point is 23 degrees 51 minutes, which is very large. The Zodiac starting with the fixed star point is called the fixed Zodiac or Sidereal Zodiac. The Hindus all through followed this Zodiac and for all

Astrological purposes used this Zodiac only. Many in the West, since the 3rd century AD., following an Astrological work written by Ptolomy, the Greek Astronomer-Astrologer used the Zodiac based on the Vernal Equinox as starting point. The starting point of this Zodiac however changes every year. Hence this is called the moving Zodiac or Tropical Zodiac.

Since all planetary positions are given in longitude of degrees, minutes and seconds measured from the zero starting point of the Zodiac, these longitudes are different in the two systems. The tropical Zodiac has a starting point much behind the fixed Zodiac. Hence the Planetary Longitudinal Values according to the Tropical system will be higher than those of the Sidereal. So from the Tropical if you have to get the Sidereal you will have to DEDUCT the value by which the equinox has moved away behind the fixed point. This value is called precession of the Equinox, the AYANAMSA.

In this book explaining Vedic astrological comparison of charts only Sidereal, that is, fixed Zodiac is used. If you have your horoscope in the Vedic system you can use the same. If you have your horoscope according to the Western system, it can be easily converted to the fixed Zodiac system. From each of the longitudes of the Ascendant and the nine planets DEDUCT the Ayanamsa for the year of birth and you will get the Longitudes of the planets and the Ascendant as per the fixed Zodiac.

I have given in the following table, the 'Ayanamsa' for all years from 1900 to 2050 :

(See Table of 'Ayanamsa' on page no. 34)

TABLE OF AYANAMSA

(CHITRA PAKSHA AYANAMSA *)

Difference between Tropical and Sidereal longitudes as on 15th April of each year

Aynamsa		Aynamsa		Aynamsa		Aynamsa	
Year	**d° m' s"**	**Year**	**d° m' s"**	**Year**	**d° m's"**	**Year**	**d° m' s"**
1900	22 2810.1535	1938	23 0000.0531	1976	23 3150.2733	2014	24 03 40.8226
1901	22 2900.4099	1939	23 0950.3180	1977	23 3240.5468	2015	24 04 31.1045
1902	22 2950.6665	1940	23 0140.5831	1978	23 3330.8206	2016	24 05 21.3866
1903	22 3040.9233	1941	23 0230.8484	1979	23 3421.0946	2017	24 06 11.6690
1904	22 3131.1804	1942	23 0321.1139	1980	23 3511.3688	2018	24 07 01.9516
1905	22 3221.4377	1943	23 0411.3796	1981	23 3601.6432	2019	24 07 52.2344
1906	22 3311.6952	1944	23 0501.6456	1982	23 3651.9178	2020	24 08 42.5174
1907	22 3401.9529	1945	23 0551.9118	1983	23 3742.1927	2021	24 09 32.8006
1908	22 3452.2109	1946	23 0642.1782	1984	23 3832.4678	2022	24 10 23.0841
1909	22 3542.4691	1947	23 0732.4448	1985	23 3922.7431	2023	24 11 13.3679
1910	22 3632.7275	1948	23 0822.7116	1986	23 4013.0186	2024	24 12 03.6519
1911	22 3722.9861	1949	23 0912.9787	1987	23 4103.2943	2025	24 12 53.9361
1912	22 3813.2449	1950	23 1003.2460	1988	23 4153.5703	2026	24 13 44.2205
1913	22 3903.5039	1951	23 1053.5135	1989	23 4243.8465	2027	24 14 34.5051
1914	22 3953.7632	1952	23 1143.7813	1990	23 4334.1229	2028	24 15 24.7900
1915	22 4044.0227	1953	23 1234.0491	1991	23 4424.3925	2029	24 16 16.0751
1916	22 4134.2824	1954	23 1324.3173	1992	23 4514.6763	2030	24 17 05.3604
1917	22 4224.5423	1955	23 1414.5857	1993	23 4604.9534	2031	24 17 55.6459
1918	22 4314.8024	1956	23 1504.8543	1994	23 4655.2307	2032	24 18 45.9316
1919	22 4405.0628	1957	23 1555.1232	1995	23 4745.5[illegible]2	2033	24 19 36.2176
1920	22 4455.3234	1958	23 1645.3922	1996	23 4835.7859	2034	24 20 26.5038
1921	22 4545.5842	1959	23 1735.6615	1997	23 4926.0638	2035	24 21 16.7902
1922	22 4635.8453	1960	23 1825.9310	1998	23 5016.3420	2036	24 22 07.0768
1923	22 4726.1066	1961	23 1916.2077	1999	23 5106.6204	2037	24 22 57.3636
1924	22 4816.3682	1962	23 2006.4706	2000	23 5156.8990	2038	24 23 47.6507
1925	22 4906.6300	1963	23 2056.7407	2001	23 5247.1778	2039	24 24 37.9380
1926	22 4956.8920	1964	23 2147.0111	2002	23 5337.4568	2040	24 25 28.2225
1927	22 5047.1542	1965	23 2237.2817	2003	23 5427.7361	2041	24 26 18.5132
1928	22 5137.4166	1966	23 2327.5525	2004	23 5518.0156	2042	24 27 08.8011
1929	22 5227.6793	1967	23 2417.8235	2005	23 5608.2953	2043	24 27 58.0893
1930	22 5317.9422	1968	23 2508.0947	2006	23 5658.5752	2044	24 28 49.3777
1931	22 5408.2853	1969	23 2558.3662	2007	23 5748.8554	2045	24 29 39.6663
1932	22 5458.4686	1970	23 2648.6379	2008	23 5839.1378	2046	24 30 29.9551
1933	22 5548.7321	1971	23 2738.9098	2009	23 5929.4164	2047	24 31 20.2441
1934	22 5638.9959	1972	23 2829.1820	2010	24 0019.6972	2048	24 32 10.5334
1935	22 5729.2599	1973	23 2919.4544	2011	24 0109.9782	2049	24 33 00.8229
1936	22 5819.5241	1974	23 3009.7271	2012	24 0200.2594	2050	24 33 51.1126
1937	22 5909.7885	1975	23 3100.0000	2013	24 0250.5409		

* *It is the most widely accepted "AYANAMSA" value.*

YOUR SIDEREAL CHART FROM YOUR TROPICAL CHART

FIRST TABULATE THE LONGITUDES OF THE ASCENDANT AND THE PLANETS IN DEGREES AND MINUTES:

EXAMPLE: Female Born on 11-03-1948, at 11h-35m. Indian Standard Time or 6h-05m G.M.T. at Long. 70°-56' East and Lat.: 22°-18' North.

(Indian Standard Time = G.M.T.+ 5h-30m)

Tropical Longitudes

Ascendant	:	Scorpio	:	25° - 38'
Sun	:	Pisces	:	21° - 05'
Moon	:	Aries	:	0° - 47'
Mars	:	Cancer	:	20° - 07'
Mercury	:	Aquarius	:	24° - 21'
Jupiter	:	Sagittarius	:	27° - 08'
Venus	:	Taurus	:	3° - 58'
Saturn	:	Cancer	:	16° - 56'
Rahu	:	Taurus	:	17° - 05'
Ketu	:	Scorpio	:	17° - 05'

From Table you will note the Ayanamsa for the year 1948 is 23°- 08'.

This value has to be deducted from each of the above longitudes to obtain the Sidereal Longitudes. On deduction we have :

Ascendant	:	Scorpio	:	2° - 30'
Sun	:	Aquarius	:	27° - 57'
Moon	:	Pisces	:	7° - 39'
Mars	:	Gemini	:	26° - 59'
Mercury	:	Aquarius	:	1° - 13'
Jupiter	:	Sagittarius	:	4° - 00'
Venus	:	Aries	:	10° - 50'
Saturn	:	Gemini	:	23° - 08'
Rahu	:	Aries	:	23° - 57'
Ketu	:	Libra	:	23° - 57'

The Ascendant and planets are then placed in the corresponding signs as shown in the following figures. This is the main chart to work out the comparison.

SIMPLE CIRCULAR RASHI CHART

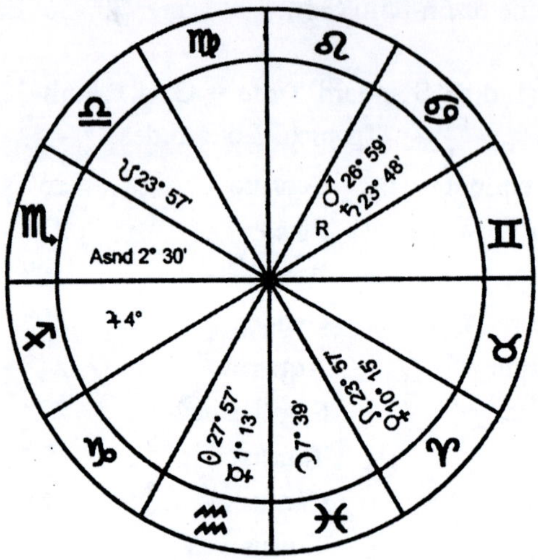

RASHI CHART USED IN SOUTH INDIA

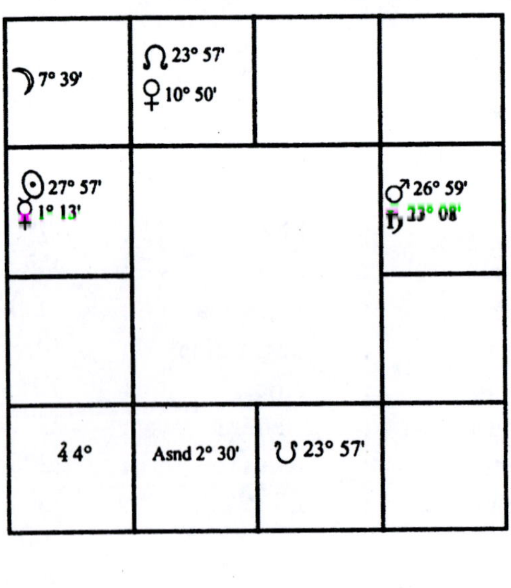

NAKSHATRAS

In Vedic Astrology, the Zodiac is divided into 27 parts called Nakshatras or Lunar Mansions. Since it takes about 27⅓ days for the Moon to go round the entire Zodiac, the Zodiac is divided into 27 parts starting from 0° Aries (Mesham). The Moon would therefore take approximately one day to move through one Nakshatra. These twenty-seven divisions are given names just as we have given names for the twelve signs of the Zodiac.

Names of the 27 Nakshatras :

Nos.	Nakshatras	Nos.	Nakshatras
1.	ASHWINI	15.	SWATI
2.	BHARANI	16.	VISHAKHA
3.	KRITTIKA	17.	ANURADHA
4.	ROHINI	18.	JYESHTHA
5.	MRIGASHIRA	19.	MOOLA
6.	ARDRA	20.	POORVA ASHADHA
7.	PUNARVASU	21.	UTTARA ASHADHA
8.	PUSHYA	22.	SHRAVANA
9.	ASHLESHA	23.	DHANISHTHA
10.	MAGHA	24.	SHATABHISHA
11.	POORVA PHALGUNI	25.	POORVA BHADRA
12.	UTTARA PHALGUNI	26.	UTTARA BHADRA
13.	HASTA	27.	REVATI
14.	CHITRA		

Note that in the system explained in this book only the number of the Nakshatra is used and the difficult Sanskrit names need not be learnt by heart by non professionals. The next table gives the planet that rules the Nakshatra and the orb (range) of each Nakshatra in the Zodiac signs.

No.	Name of Nakshatra	Planetary Ruler	Range	Sign
1	Ashwini	Ketu	00-00–13°-20'	Aries
2	Bharani	Venus	13°-20'–26°-40'	Aries
3	Krittika	Sun	26°-40'–10°-00'	Aries-Taurus
4	Rohini	Moon	10°-00'–23°-20'	Taurus
5	Mrigashira	Mars	23°-20'–06°-40'	Taurus-Gemini
6	Ardra	Rahu	06°-40'–20°-00'	Gemini
7	Punarvasu	Jupiter	20°-00'–03°-20'	Gemini-Cancer
8	Pushya	Saturn	03°-20'–16°-40'	Cancer
9	Ashlesha	Mercury	16°-40'–30°-00'	Cancer
10	Magha	Ketu	00°-00'–13°-20'	Leo
11	Poorva Phalguni	Venus	13°-20'–26°-40'	Leo
12	Uttara Phalguni	Sun	26°-40'–10°-00'	Leo-Virgo
13	Hasta	Moon	10°-00'–23°-20'	Virgo
14	Chitra	Mars	23°-20'–06°-40'	Virgo-Libra
15	Swati	Rahu	06°-40'–20°-00'	Libra
16	Vishakha	Jupiter	20°-00'–03°-20'	Libra-Scorpio
17	Anuradha	Saturn	03°-20'–16°-40'	Scorpio
18	Jyeshtha	Mercury	16°-40'–30°-00'	Scorpio
19	Moola	Ketu	00-00'–13°-20'	Sagittarius
20	Poorva Ashadha	Venus	13°-20'–26°-40'	Sagittarius
21	Uttara Ashadha	Sun	26°-40'–10°-00'	Sagi-Capricorn
22	Shravana	Moon	10°-00'–23°-20'	Capricorn
23	Dhanishtha	Mars	23°-20'–06°-40'	Capri-Aquarius
24	Shatabhisha	Rahu	06°-40'–20°-00'	Aquarius
25	Poorva Bhadra	Jupiter	20°-00'–03°-20'	Aqua-Pisces
26	Uttara Bhadra	Saturn	03°-20'–16°-40'	Pisces
27	Revati	Mercury	16°-40'–30°-00'	Pisces

PADAS

Since the Zodiac of 360 degrees are divided into 27 parts, each Nakshatra is of 13°-20'. Now again each nakshatra is divided into four parts which are called PADAS (literal meaning is *feet*). Each pada is therefore 3°-20'. There are no individual names for the padas. They are only referred as the first, second, third and fourth padas of that particular Nakshatra. But these padas have planetary rulers.

Starting from the first pada of the first Nakshatra (Ashwini) the padas are designated the same rulers of the twelve Zodiac Signs in the same order. Thus the first pada of the first Nakshatra is ruled by Mars (Kuja), the ruler of Aries. The second pada is ruled by Venus, the ruler of Taurus, the third pada by Mercury, the ruler of Gemini and the fourth pada by Moon, the ruler of Cancer. Continuing we have the first pada of the second nakshatra (Bharani) ruled by Sun, the ruler of Leo, the second pada ruled by Mercury, ruler of Virgo, the third pada ruled by Venus the ruler of Libra and the fourth pada ruled by mars the ruler of Scorpio. The four padas of the third Nakshatra (Krittika) are ruled by Jupiter, Saturn, Saturn and Jupiter respectively being the rulers of Sagittarius, Capricorn, Aquarius and Pisces. The first pada of the fourth Nakshatra (Rohini) naturally will have ruler Mars, the ruler of Aries.

It can be seen that the rulers of the twelve signs of the Zodiac rule the twelve padas of the first three Nakshatras and from the fourth again the rulers of the Zodiac repeat themselves. Since there are 27 Nakshatras with 4 padas each, we have totally 108 padas in the Zodiac. The twelve rulers of the Zodiac signs therefore repeat themselves as rulers of the padas nine times. The figure on the next page gives this arrangement of the 360° Zodiac, in the anti clockwise direction, with the 12 signs in three groups of four signs shown by sides of the triangle, The 27 Nakshatra divisions and their rulers, the 108 padas and their ruling planet zodiac signs.

NAKSHATRA MANDALA						
	Nakshatra	Pada 1.	Pada 2.	Pada 3.	Pada 4.	
		sign/ruler	sign/ruler	sign/ruler	sign/ruler	Group
1	Ashwini	Aries/Mras	Tau/Venu	Gem/Merc	Cancer/Moon	G 1
2	Bharani	Leo/Sun	Virgo/Merc	Libra/Ven	Scorp/Mars	G 2
3	Krittika	Sagi/Jup	Capri/Sat	Aqua/Sat	Pisces/Jup	G 3
4	Rohini	Aries/Mars	Tau/Venus	Gem/Merc	Cancer/Moon	G 1
5	Mrigashira	Leo/Sun	Virgo/Mercu	Libra/Venus	Scor/Mars	G 2
6	Ardra	Sagit/Jup	Capri/Sat	Aqua/Sat	Pisces/Jup	G 3
7	Punarvasu	Aries/Mars	Tau/Venu	Gemi.Merc	Cancer/Moon	G 1
8	Pushya	Leo/Sun	Virgo/Merc	Libra/Venus	Scor/Mars	G 2
9	Ashlesha	Sagi/Jup	Capri/Sat	Aqua/Sat	Pisces/Jup	G 3
10	Magha	Aries/Mars	Tau/Venus	Gem/Merc	Cancer/Moon	G 1
11	Poorva Phalguni	Leo/Sun	Virgo/Merc	Libra/Venus	Scor/Mars	G 2
12	Uttara Phalguni	Sagi/Jup	Capri/Sat	Aqua/Sat	Pisces/Jup	G 3
13	Hasta	Aries/Mars	Tau/Venus	Gem/Merc	Cancer/Moon	G 1
14	Chitra	Leo/Sun	Virgo/Mercu	Libra/Venus	Scor/Mars	G 2
15	Swati	Sagit/Jup	Capri/Sat	Aqua/Sat	Pisces/Jup	G 3
16	Vishakha	Aries/Mars	Tau/Venus	Gemi/Merc	Cancer/Moon	G 1
17	Anuradha	Leo/Sun	Virgo/Merc	Libra/Venus	Scor/Mars	G 2
18	Jyeshtha	Sagi/Jup	Capri/Sat	Aqua/Sat	Pisces/Jup	G 3
19	Moola	Aries/Mars	Tau/Venus	Gem/Merc	Cancer/Moon	G 1
20	Poorva Ashadha	Leo/Sun	Virgo/Merc	Libra/Venus	Scor/Mars	G 2
21	Uttara Ashadha	Sagi/Jup	Capri/Sat	Aqua/Sat	Pisces/Jup	G 3
22	Shravana	Aries/Mars	Tau/Venus	Gem/Merc	Cancer/Moon	G 1
23	Dhanishtha	Leo/Sun	Virgo/Merc	Libra/Venus	Scor/Mars	G 2
24	Shatabhisha	Sagi/Jup	Capri/Sat	Aqua/Sat	Pisces/Jup	G 3
25	Poorva Bhadra	Aries/Mars	Tau/Venus	Gem/Merc	Cancer/Moon	G 1
26	Uttara Bhadra	Leo/Sun	Virgo/Merc	Libra/Venus	Scor/Mars	G 2
27	Revati	Sagi/Jup	Capri/Sat	Aqua/Sat	Pisces/Jup	G 3

GROUPING OF NAKSHATRAS

1. GROUP 1. (G.1)

1. Ashwini	10. Magha	19. Moola
4. Rohini	13. Hasta	22. Shravana
7. Punarvasu	16. Vishakha	25. Poorva Bhadra

From the figure you will note that these 9 Nakshatras have the same signs Aries, Taurus, Gemini and Cancer and therefore the same rulers allotted respectively to the first, second, third and fourth padas. Also Nakshatras 1, 10, 19 are ruled by Ketu, 4, 13, 22 by Moon and 7, 16, 25 by Jupiter.

2. GROUP 2. (G.2)

2. Bharani	11. Poorva Phalguni	20. Poorva Ashadha
5. Mrigashira	14. Chitra	23. Dhanishtha
8. Pushya	17. Anuradha	26. Uttara Bhadra

These Nakshatras are grouped together as their four padas are ruled by Leo, Virgo, Libra and Scorpio, whose planetary rulers are Sun, Mercury, Venus and Mars respectively. The Nakshatras 2, 11, 20 are ruled by Venus, Nakshatras 5, 14, 23 by Mars and 8, 17, 26 by Saturn.

3. GROUP 3. (G.3)

3. Krittika	12. Uttara Phalguni	21. Uttara Ashadha
6. Ardra	15. Swati	24. Shatabhisha
9. Ashlesha	18. Jyeshtha	27. Revati

These Nakshatras have their four padas allotted to Sagittarius, Capricorn, Aquarius and Pisces whose rulers are Jupiter, Saturn, Saturn and Jupiter respectively. The Nakshatras 3, 12, 21 are ruled by Sun, 6, 15, 24 ruled by Rahu and 9, 18, 27 are ruled by Mercury.

I have found that this grouping of Nakshatras based on same set of Pada rulers is important for some of the rules given by the sages.

THE PLANETS

Signs	♈	♉	♊	♋	♌	♍	♎	♏	♐	♑	♒	♓
Lords	♂	♀	☿	☽	☉	☿	♀	♂	♃	♄	♄	♃
Exaltations	☉ 10	☽ 3		♃ 5		☿ 15	♄ 20			♂ 28		♀ 27
Debilitations	♄ 20			♂ 28		♀ 27	☉ 10	☽ 3		♃ 5		☿ 15
Moola Trikona	♂ 0-18	☽ 4-20			☉ 0-20	☿ 16-20	♀ 0-10		♃ 0-13		♄ 0-20	

In the above table the first row gives the Zodiac Signs, the second the planets that rule the sign, the third, the planet that is exalted in the sign.

A planet is strongest when it is in its sign of exaltation. The sages have also given specific degree in that sign at which the planet is most positive. Naturally at the exact opposite point in the Zodiac it is debilitated.

A planet is strong when it is in the sign it rules. As you can see from the table, some planets rule two signs. A planet ruling two signs is relatively strong in one of the two signs it rules. This sign is called its MOOLA TRIKONA sign and is indicated as M.T. in some tables. Mars rules Aries and Scorpio and is relatively strong in Aries. In other words the positive qualities of a planet are enhanced in its Moola Trikona sign. Sun rules only one sign Leo and that sign is also its Moola Trikona sign. Moon also rules only one sign Cancer. But sages have said that its Moola Trikona sign is Taurus where indeed it is exalted and most powerful at the 3rd degree of this sign.

In matrimonial comparison normally the exact degree of exaltation or debilitation, where the maximum effect is felt, is not necessarily taken into consideration. We only consider whether the planet is in its sign of exaltation or debilitation.

PLANETARY RELATIONSHIPS

1. Natural

In Vedic Astrology, there is mutual relationship between planets. The nature of energies of a planet are harmonious with some planets and incompatible with some others and neutral with some. The following table gives the relationships considered as friendly, neutral and inimical.

Planet	Friend	Neutral	Enemy
Sun	Mar, Moon, Jup	Mer	Ven, Sat
Moon	Sun, Mer, Ven	Mar, Jup, Sat	
Mars	Sun, Moon, Jup	Ven, Sat	Mer
Mercury	Sun, Venus	Mar, Jup, Sat	Moon
Jupiter	Sun, Moon, Mar	Sat	Mer, Ven
Venus	Mer, Sat	Mar, Jup	Sun, Moon
Saturn	Mer, Ven	Jup	Sun, Moon, Mar
Rahu	Mer, Ven, Sat	Jup	Sun, Moon, Mar
Ketu	Mars, Jup, Sun, Moon	Sat, Ven	Mer

2. Temporary

Besides the above Natural Relationship between planets, Vedic Astrology mentions about Temporary Relationships between planets. The distance between one planet and another in the Zodiac has an effect on the harmony between the planets. Thus distance is considered by sign position. The following table gives this relationship. There is no neutral relationship here.

RULE

Temporary Friend of a planet	Temporary Enemy of a planet
Planets in the 2, 3, 4, 10, 11, 12 signs from its sign	Planets in the 1, 5, 6, 7, 8, 9 signs from its sign

In any horoscope chart the two relationships exist between the planets and the net relationship has to be used. Combining the two we can have a total of six possible relationships. As for example in a chart a planet is a Natural friend and also a Temporary Friend of another planet. We can say in that chart it is a Grand Friend of the other planet. Thus we have:

1.	Natural Friend	+	Temporary Friend	=	Very Friendly
2.	Natural Friend	+	Temporary Enemy	=	Neutral
3.	Neutral	+	Temporary Friend	=	Friend
4.	Neutral	+	Temporary Enemy	=	Enemy
5.	Natural Enemy	+	Temporary Friend	=	Neutral
6.	Natural Enemy	+	Temporary Enemy	=	Very Inimical

EXAMPLE:

Person born on 1-7-1961 at 18h-45m GMT, at Lat. 52°-50' N, Long. 0°-30' E

		Venus 1°-05'	Mercury 9°-55' Sun 16°-21'
Moon 1°-41' Ketu 6°-24'			
Saturn 4°-49' Jupiter 11°-44'			Rahu 6°-24' Mars 8°-20'
	Asnd 25°-08'		

1. Sun is in the sign ruled by Mercury, Natural Neutral and Mercury being in the 1st sign from Sun is a Temporary Enemy. Net result in this chart : Sun is in enemy place.
2. Saturn is in Capricorn owned by itself. So net does not arise.
3. Rahu is in the sign of Sun, Natural Enemy and Sun is situated in 11th sign from it. So its is a Temporary Friend.Net = Neutral.
4. Ketu is in the sign of Saturn, a Natural Neutral and since Saturn is situated in the 12 from it, is a Temporary Friend.
   Net = Friend.

5. Mars is in the sign of Sun a Natural Friend and since Sun is placed in the 11th from it becomes a Temporary Friend. Net = Very Friendly.

RASHI AND NAKSHATRAS

Since the Zodiac is divided into twelve signs, called RASHI in Sanskrit and into twenty seven parts called NAKSHATRAS, each planet obviously is in a particular sign and a particular Nakshatra. In Vedic Astrology the RASHI and NAKSHATRA in which Moon (Chandra) is placed in a horoscope is important. Just as the Sun Sign plays an important part in Western Astrology, the RASHI*, that is the Moon Sign and NAKSHATRA play an important role in Vedic Astrology. When a person in India is asked what Rashi or Nakshatra he or she belongs to the reference is only to the Rashi and Nakshatra in which Moon is situated in the birth chart. So in this book whenever we refer to the Rashi and Nakshatra of a person it usually means the Sign and Nakshatra division in which Moon is in the persons birth chart.

BHAVA (HOUSES)

The Birth Chart is also divided into twelve Bhavas or Houses. In the Vedic system the degree of the Ascendant or Lagna is considered the MID POINT of the First house. The first house therefore extends from fifteen degrees behind this point to fifteen degrees in front so that the house is of thirty degrees. For example if the Ascendant is 18°-20' of Cancer, the first house extends from 3°-20' of Cancer to 3°-20' of Leo. Having marked the first house, every thirty degrees is marked off making twelve equal houses. This is known as equal house division. There are other systems of house division also which however are not explained in this sandwich course.

The Bhavas or Houses are related to different departments of life. I give briefly the different departments of life that come under each house. The list is not exhaustive. I have given only those that may be relevant for the purpose of comparison of charts for relationship.

---

* *Generally in the Vedic system the Birth Chart is referred as RASHI CHAKRA and the Moon sign as RASHI for a person.*

First House: This house is connected with character, personality, physical features, general health, longevity and good fortune in general.

Second House: It is connected with income, finance, source of earning. In Vedic Astrology this is also connected with speech and nature of death, family happiness and longevity of life partner.

Third House: Mental qualities, courage and confidence, travel, brothers and sisters and longevity.

Fourth House: Domestic environment, domestic relationships, properties, comforts in life, education, mother.

Fifth House: Love and romance, emotional and sentimental affairs, birth and rapport with children, pleasures, luxuries and enjoyments in life, creativity and skills.

Sixth House: This house is connected with health, enemies and debts.

Seventh House: Marriage, matrimonial happiness and success, life partner, fruitfulness of partnership relations, dealings with the opposite sex. It is also called the place of death as it indicates the nature of ones death being exactly opposite to the ascendant related to the birth.

Eight House: This is connected with longevity, health and well-being and the nature of death of the life partner.

Ninth House: Related to higher knowledge, good fortune, foreign travel, religious affairs and spirituality.

Tenth House: Matters related to profession, fame and vocational activities.

Eleventh House: Matters related to friends, social contacts and profit in enterprises.

Twelfth House: Indicates obstructions in life, difficulties, sorrows and sufferings, restrictions, pleasures of the bed, secret relationship, loss of limbs, possibilities of loss of life partner.

BENEFIC AND MALEFIC PLANETS

In Vedic Astrology, we have Natural Benefic and Natural Malefic planets. *It is important to note that this division is only for the purpose of evolving a technique to judge the effects of planets in a particular horoscope. In fact all planets are capable of giving positive and negative results as a consequence to the specific configuration in a chart.* There is noting absolute about this classification. It is a basic classification which serves as a starting point for assessing a planet which may eventually be the opposite to its basic classification.

NATURAL BENEFIC PLANETS: JUPITER, VENUS, WAXING MOON AND MERCURY NOT ASSOCIATED (IN THE SAME SIGN) WITH ANY MALEFIC.

NATURAL MALEFIC PLANETS: SATURN, MARS, SUN, RAHU, KETU, WANING MOON AND MERCURY ASSOCIATED WITH A MALEFIC.

SOME MODIFICATIONS: In a chart the planets ruling the 1st, 4th, 5th, 7th, 9th, 10th are considered benefic for that chart (even though some of them happen to be naturally malefic). The planets ruling the 3rd, 6th, 8th and 12th houses are considered malefic for the chart (even though some of them may be naturally benefic). Thus in a particular horoscope on account of being the ruler of a house the basic classification changes.

PLANETARY PERIODS

In Vedic Astrology, there is a system of calculating periods of life ruled by a planet. The system is based on the position of Moon in the Nakshatra at birth. Each Nakshatra has a planetary ruler. When a person is born in a Nakshatra, the planet ruling that Nakshatra is the planet ruling at the time of the birth. Then the cycles follow starting from that planet. First it is important to know how many years of life each planet rules. Taking a life covered by all the nine planetary cycles as 120 years, the sages allotted the period as follows.

Vimsottari Dasha - Planetary Cycles in a life of 120 years. Presuming normal human longevity is 120 years, in the system called Vimsottari dasha in Vedic astrology each planet has a certain number of years it rules.

- Sun 6 years
- Moon 10 Years
- Mars 7 Years
- Rahu 18 years
- Jupiter 16 years
- Saturn 19 years
- Mercury 17 years
- Ketu 7 years
- Venus 20 years

Total life cycle 120 years. The planetary cycles follow a specific order as follows:

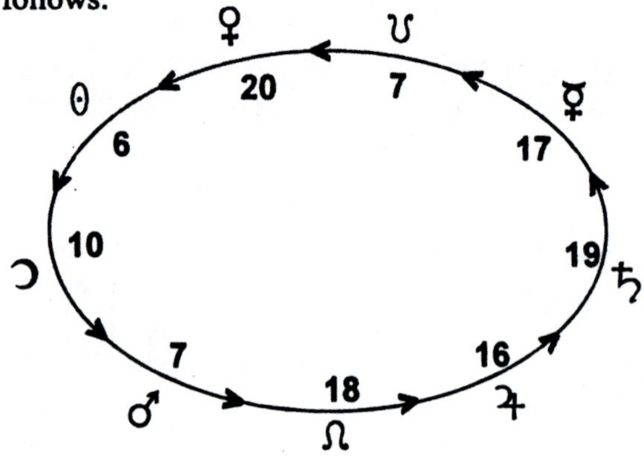

The number of years and the Cyclic order of Sun-Moon-Mars-Rahu-Jupiter-Saturn-Mercury-Ketu-Venus is the same for everyone. The difference is that each one starts at a different point in this cycle. First we have to find the Planetary Cycle at the time of birth and the number of years of that cycle elapsed in the prenatal stage. This depends on the longitude of the Moon at the time of birth. We have seen that each Nakshatra is ruled by a planet. The cycle at birth is the cycle of the planet ruling the Nakshatra in which the Moon is at the time of birth. We know that each Nakshatra has a longitude of 13°-20'. This length is proportionate to the number of years of the planet ruling the Nakshatra. The length through which the Moon has moved in the Nakshatra at birth indicated the number of years elapsed before birth.

EXAMPLE:

Let us presume in a particular horoscope Moon is 6°-40' in Leo. We note from the table of Nakshatras that this falls in the Nakshatra Magha which is the 10th Nakshatra ruled by Ketu. So the planetary period at birth is Ketu. However this Nakshatra extends from 0° to 13°-20' of Leo. But Moon is at 6°-40', which is the mid point of this orb.

Hence out of 7 years of Ketu, 3½ years are over before birth and 3½ years remain. This is the remaining part of the first planetary cycle (DASHA) to be gone through. Then the planetary cycle to follow would be Venus 20 years, Sun 6 years and so on. It is not implied that a person will live through all the cycles and reach the ripe old age of 120 though it is not ruled out either. Only the sequence of planetary cycles are given.

In our example we have taken the case where the longitude of Moon is exactly mid way the orb of the Nakshatra. This is only convenience. But it can be any degree. The proportion of the remaining period has to be calculated mathematically by the rule of proportion.

However to make the calculation easy I have included the standard ready-reckoner which will enable one to find the balance of DASHA at birth once you know the degree of Moon in the birth chart.

Tables 1 and 2 have to be used. Table 1 shows on the top row the twelve Zodiac signs in four columns each having three signs. The left column gives the longitude of Moon from 0° to 29°- 40'.

In Table 2 we have the planets in the order of the DASHA cycles and the number of years for each cycle given on the top row. The first and last column give minutes of Moons longitude from 1' to 30'.

Table - 1

Position of the Moon	♈ ♌ ♐			♉ ♍ ♑			♊ ♎ ♒			♋ ♏ ♓		
Deg. Mts.	**y**	**m**	**d**	**y**	**m**	**d**	**y**	**m**	**d**	**y**	**m**	**d**
00 00	*Ketu* 7	0	0	*Sun* 4	6	0	*Mars* 3	6	0	*Jupiter* 4	0	0
01 00	6	5	21	4	0	18	2	11	21	2	9	18
02 00	5	11	12	3	1	24	1	11	3	0	4	24
03 00	5	5	3	3	1	24	1	11	3	0	4	24
03 20	5	3	0	3	0	0	1	9	0	*Sat-* 19	0	0
04 00	4	10	25	2	8	12	1	4	24	*urn*18	0	18
05 00	4	4	15	2	3	0	0	10	15	16	7	15
06 00	3	10	6	1	9	18	0	4	6	15	2	12
06 40	3	6	0	1	6	0	*Rahu* 18	0	0	14	3	0
07 00	3	3	27	1	4	6	17	6	18	13	9	9
08 00	2	9	18	0	10	24	16	2	12	12	4	6
09 00	2	3	9	0	5	12	14	10	6	10	11	3
10 00	1	9	0	*Moon* 10	0	0	13	6	0	9	6	0
11 00	1	2	21	9	3	0	12	1	24	8	0	27
12 00	0	8	12	8	6	0	10	9	18	6	7	24
13 00	0	2	3	7	9	0	9	5	12	5	2	21
13 20	*Venus* 20	0	0	7	6	0	9	8	0	4	9	0
14 00	19	0	0	7	0	0	8	1	6	3	9	8
15 00	17	6	0	6	3	0	6	9	0	2	4	15
16 00	16	0	0	5	6	0	5	4	24	0	11	12
16 40	15	0	0	5	0	0	4	6	0	*Mer-* 17	0	0
17 00	14	6	0	4	9	0	4	0	18	*cury* 16	6	27
18 00	13	0	0	4	0	0	2	8	12	15	3	18
19 00	11	6	0	3	3	0	1	4	6	14	0	9
20 00	10	0	0	2	6	0	*Jupiter* 16	8	0	12	9	0
21 00	8	6	0	1	9	0	14	9	18	11	5	21
22 00	7	0	0	1	0	0	13	7	6	10	2	12
23 00	5	6	0	0	3	0	12	4	24	8	11	3
23 20	5	0	0	*Mars* 7	0	0	12	0	0	8	6	0
24 00	4	0	0	6	7	24	11	2	12	7	7	24
25 00	2	6	0	6	1	15	10	0	0	6	4	15
26 00	1	0	0	5	7	6	8	9	18	5	1	6
26 40	*Sun* 6	0	0	5	3	0	8	0	0	4	3	0
27 00	5	10	6	5	0	27	7	7	6	3	9	27
28 00	5	4	24	4	6	18	6	4	24	2	6	18
29 00	4	11	12	4	0	9	5	2	12	1	3	9
29 20	4	9	18	3	10	6	4	9	18	0	10	6
29 40	4	7	24	3	8	3	4	4	24	0	5	3

Table - 2

	7Y		♀ 20Y		θ 6Y		ↄ 10Y		♂ 7Y		☊ 18Y		♃ 16Y		♄ 19Y		☿ 17Y		
Min	**m**	**d**	**m**	**d**	**m**	**d**	**m**	**d**	**m**	**d**	**m**	**d**	**m**	**d**	**m**	**d**	**m**	**d**	**Min**
1	0	3	0	9	0	3	0	5	0	3	0	8	0	7	0	9	0	8	1
2	0	6	0	18	0	5	0	9	0	6	0	16	0	14	0	17	0	15	2
3	0	9	0	27	0	8	0	14	0	9	0	24	0	22	0	26	0	23	3
4	0	13	1	6	0	11	0	18	0	13	1	2	0	29	1	4	1	1	4
5	0	16	1	15	0	14	0	23	0	16	1	11	1	6	1	13	1	8	5
6	0	19	1	24	0	16	0	27	0	19	1	19	1	13	1	21	1	16	6
7	0	22	2	3	0	19	1	27	0	22	1	27	1	20	2	0	1	24	7
8	0	25	2	12	0	22	1	16	0	25	2	5	1	28	2	8	2	1	8
9	0	28	2	21	0	24	1	11	0	28	2	13	2	5	2	17	2	9	9
10	1	1	3	0	0	27	1	15	1	1	2	21	2	12	2	26	2	17	10
11	1	4	3	9	1	0	1	20	1	4	2	29	2	19	3	5	2	25	11
12	1	7	3	18	1	2	1	24	1	7	3	7	2	26	3	13	3	2	12
13	1	10	3	27	1	5	4	29	1	10	3	15	3	4	3	22	3	10	13
14	1	14	4	6	1	8	2	3	1	14	3	23	3	11	4	0	3	18	14
15	1	17	4	15	1	11	2	8	1	17	3	2	3	18	4	8	3	25	15
16	1	20	4	24	1	14	2	13	1	20	4	10	3	25	4	17	4	3	16
17	1	23	5	3	1	16	2	17	1	23	4	18	4	2	4	5	4	10	17
18	1	26	5	12	1	19	2	22	1	26	4	26	4	10	5	4	4	18	18
19	2	0	5	21	1	22	2	26	2	0	5	4	4	17	5	12	4	26	19
20	2	3	6	0	1	24	3	0	2	3	5	12	4	24	5	21	5	3	20
21	2	6	6	9	1	27	3	5	2	6	5	20	5	1	6	0	5	11	21
22	2	9	6	18	1	29	3	9	2	9	5	28	5	8	6	8	5	18	22
23	2	12	6	27	2	2	3	14	2	22	6	6	5	16	6	17	5	26	23
24	2	16	7	6	2	5	3	18	2	16	6	14	5	23	6	25	6	4	24
25	2	19	7	15	2	8	3	23	2	19	6	23	6	0	7	4	6	11	25
26	2	22	7	24	2	10	3	27	2	22	7	1	6	7	7	12	6	19	26
27	2	25	8	3	2	13	4	2	2	25	7	9	6	14	7	21	6	27	27
28	2	28	8	12	2	16	4	6	2	28	7	17	6	22	7	29	7	4	28
29	3	1	8	21	2	18	4	11	3	1	7	25	6	29	8	8	7	12	29
30	3	4	9	0	2	21	4	15	3	4	8	3	7	6	8	17	7	20	30

USE OF TABLES 1 and 2

EXAMPLE 1:

Presume in a horoscope Moon is 26°-10' in Virgo.

In Table 1 we have Virgo in the second column. Now find 26° looking down the first column. Opposite to 26° in the second column we find Mars Dasha 5 years 7 months 6 days. We do not have 26°-10'. The nearest is 26°.

For the 10' we take Table 2. Under the head Mars (7Y) we find on the row opposite 10' the period 1 month 1 day. So this period has passed away further in the Mars cycle at birth. So from the remaining period of the cycle indicated against 26° we have to *deduct* this period. The balance of Mars cycle remaining at the time of birth is therefore 5 years 6 months and 5 days.

EXAMPLE 2:

Method 1

To find balance of birth Dasha when Moon is 12°-40' Aquarius

In Table 1 we have Aquarius in the third group column of Zodiac signs. In the row along 12° under this column we have Rahu Dasa 10y-9m-18d.

When we refer to table 2 we do not have 40' in the column of minutes. So the procedure is to find the period for 30' and then for 10' *add* both these to get the total period for 40'. This value is then *deducted* from the value of remaining cycle given for 12°.

We find for 30' under column for Rahu (18 Y) 8m-3d and for 10' we have 2m-21d. *Adding* both we have for 40' 10m-24d. This value is *deducted* from the period for 12 d.

	10y - 9m - 18d
(-)	10m - 24d
	9y - 10m - 24d

Method 2

The same result could be obtained by taking the nearest degree value in Table 1 as 13° instead of 12°.

Remaining period when Moon is at 13° is: 9y - 5m - 12d.
But Moon is 20' behind this degree. In Table 2
for 20' under column of Rahu we have : 5m - 12d

As Moon moves forward the planetary cycle
diminishes. Moon has not yet come to 13°
but is still 20' behind so the value for 20'
has to be added. On adding we have: 9y - 10m - 24d

If you add this period to the date of birth you will know when the birth cycle Rahu came to an end. Then add the planetary cycles in the natural order. After Rahu comes Jupiter 16 Y then Saturn 19 Y Mercury 17 Y etc.,

Note that in this system a month is always taken as 30 days.

PLANETARY ASPECTS

A planet at a point in the Zodiac extends influence all through the Zodiac. So each planet influences all the other planets in the Zodiac. This influence is related to the distance in degrees and minutes between the planets. This distance is termed as Aspect. For example, if a planet is 90° away from another planet, it is said that there is a square aspect between the planets. In Western astrology we have specific aspects depending upon this distance, such as degrees 30, 45, 60, 90, 120, 135, and 180 with specific names for these aspects. While these aspects exist in the Vedic system it is more comprehensive.

VEDIC ASTROLOGICAL RULE FOR ASPECTS:

RULE 1.

A planet is considered to have an aspect on all other planets placed anywhere in the Zodiac starting from 30° to 300° in front of it (in the normal direction of its movement). This means a planet does not aspect any planet within 30° in front and within 60° behind it.

However, the strength of this aspect energy is not the same at all points of the range. At some points this aspect energy is the strongest. Such an aspect is called a 'full aspect'.

RULE 2.

A planet has a full aspect on all other planets in the sign in which it is and also on the planets situated in the exactly opposite sign (180 deg.)

Besides Jupiter has a full aspect on planets situated in the 5th and 9th signs from the sign it occupies. Mars has a full aspect on all planets situated in the 4th and 8th signs from its own sign. Saturn has a full aspect on all planets situated in the 3rd and 10th signs from its own sign.

In the comparison technics described in this book we shall be using the aspects of Mars in particular as it is the most important planet in matrimonial relationships. For example, in a horoscope Mars is in the first house, that is in the same sign as the ascendant, then its full aspect energy is on the ascendant sign, the fourth, the seventh and eight signs counted from the ascendant.

IMPORTANT NOTE:

We have explained the sign divisions of the Zodiac. We have also spoken about house divisions.The reader of this book need not get confused about the sign and house divisions as in all the rules given here only sign division is considered and for all purposes the house may be considered to coincide with the sign division. For example if someone has 10° Cancer as ascendent for applying rules in this book, Cancer is considered the first house, sign Scorpio the fifth house, sign Capricorn the seventh house and so on.

PART II

THE APPROACH

CHAPTER 3

Cracks in the Mosaic

As a professional astrologer for four decades I have heard many an emotional monologue from either one of the partners, whose union had disintegrated or is on the verge of disintegration not withstanding the fact that in the first instance the marriage was contracted out of intense mutual love and the desire to be united in most of the cases.

SHE SAYS: Everything was fine for some time. Then he seemed to lose interest in me. He used to be extremely demonstrative and eager to show his love for me. Now he finds every excuse to avoid me. I suppose I have become.....

Or SHE SAYS: For six years our home was a Heaven. Then something went wrong somewhere. Now we are always swearing at each other. He becomes very violent at times. I know I love him and that he cares for me but I cannot understand what is wrong with us and why........

Or SHE SAYS: My husband was running a very successful textile business. We had all the good things of life and were very happy. Then he suddenly developed this aversion for business, Then an aversion to any type of work. We had to sell everything to survive. I have decided to leave. I cant understand why he......

Or HE SAYS: Of late she has become very touchy. She loses her temper at the least upset. She raises her voice as though I was stone deaf. It is getting on my nerves. I don't know where she is going to end up....

Or HE SAYS: Almost immediately after we got married she became weak and sick and has been so ever since. Most of the evenings we spend in the doctor's clinic. Of course, that was before we decided to live separately......

Many happy homes break up leaving a trail of misery, wounded feelings, ruptured emotions and devastated children. The instant cause or apparent cure for these situations may be found out but the question still remains why in the first instance they should have arisen at all and whether they could have been avoided. Why this stealthy eruption in a smooth relationship? Was there a disrupting force stealthily building up between the partners? Was there a gradual, imperceptible damage of the bio-magnetic or subtle energies of the couple ?

Where the mosaic once appeared harmonious, smooth and brilliant, layers (of illusions?) begin to peel off and cracks begin to surface. How do these situations develop-situations that eventually lead to the bitter end of a story which begins on a note of great optimism on a bright sunny day to the accompaniment of prayers, singing, dancing, wining and dining.

Vedic Astrology attributes this sad turn of events to the ill matching of the configuration of planets synchronizing with the births of the partners. The sages have given the technic for matching these configurations of planetary positions called birth charts of the partners and also identify the areas of possible trouble so that they can be avoided or overcome.

The technic can be used to prevent, if possible cure matrimonial maladies.

THE FIVE DIMENSIONS

Marital life is a multicolored complex mosaic. It may have different connotations for different people but the basic constituents are universal. Vedic Astrology takes into consideration all aspects of married life. When a man and woman decide to live together as husband and wife, they share their joys and sorrows, pool their resources, divide their duties and responsibilities, exchange their thoughts and feelings, seek companionship and encouragement mutually, satisfy their physical needs and in the process fulfil their obligation to the human species by producing young images of their own fulfilled selves. For a harmonious marital life the couple need to possess several characteristics that are mutually supplementary and complimentary to one another.

1. Mental: Constituting intellectual levels, aptitudes, style of living, interaction with others, handling situations, creative capabilities, attitudes and opinions.

2. Emotional: Constituting individual psychology, feelings, complexes, fears, inhibitions, frustrations, parental relationships, kindness, consideration, anger, sorrow, depressions, enthusiasm in life and also deeper subconscious motivations.
3. Material: Constituting the financial status , sources of earnings, savings and spending, possessions and properties and attitude to money and material matters.
4. Physical: Constituting sexual drives, approach to the sexual act, desire for or lack of desire for having children, the capacity to procreate and mutual physical attraction.

There should be supplementary or complimentary levels as the case may be in all these aspects to enjoy a long, happy and fulfilling matrimonial relationship. One's extravagance may be balanced by the others prudence to keep the family economy in good shape. One's love of art may supplement the other's creativity.

Vedic Astrology takes into consideration a *Fifth factor* , which indeed has an indirect bearing on all the four factors. It is the energy of *The Subtle Body. The permeating and unifying force that strengthens and stabilizes the four pillars on which marital happiness rests, namely the mental, emotional, material and physical compatibilities, is the harmony of the energy of their Subtle Bodies.*

I have explained this concept of the Subtle Body in the next chapter. To satisfy the intellectual hunger of those who desire to know about the Subtle Body I have devoted the whole of the next chapter to explain the same. To avoid exasperation of those who already know a lot about the Subtle Body. I have limited the explanation to just one chapter.

CHAPTER 4

Subtle Body - Chakras

We are all aware of our physical body that consists of bones and marrow, flesh and muscles, veins and vessels, blood and fluids, with their physiologiçal and biological functions, the nervous system and the brain with its psychological and electro-magnetic functions. But in the science of Yoga, the sages have envisaged a parallel bio-magnetic or psycho-biological body which we call significantly Subtle Body. It is not a 'body' in the common concept. I would prefer to call it the Subtle Energy Field.

SUBTLE because it is pervasive by tenuity, *ENERGY* because it is a force that acts and *FIELD* because it radiates over a certain area which includes the physical body and to some extent outside it. As such the Subtle Energy Field of a person can interact with the Subtle Energy Field of another person in close contact.

The energy in the Subtle Body has concentrated centres from which the energy radiates. The quality and quantity of this energy at these centres also varies. These centres are called *CHAKRAS.* Chakra literally means 'wheel'. In some books of Yoga these centres are referred as 'Padmas', that is Lotus. Each Chakra in the field has domain over certain parts of the physical body and over certain functions, including higher levels of mental activity such as *Ahamkara* (the Ego), *Buddhi* (discrimination) and *Manas* (recording felicity) As such the mental and emotional states and physical functions of the body are related to this Subtle Energy Field.

There are five Chakras at the physical level, one at the mental level and one at the spiritual level. They are:

1. Mooladhara **2. Swadhishthana** **3. Manipura**
4. Anahata **5. Vishuddha** **6. Ajna**
7. Sahasrara

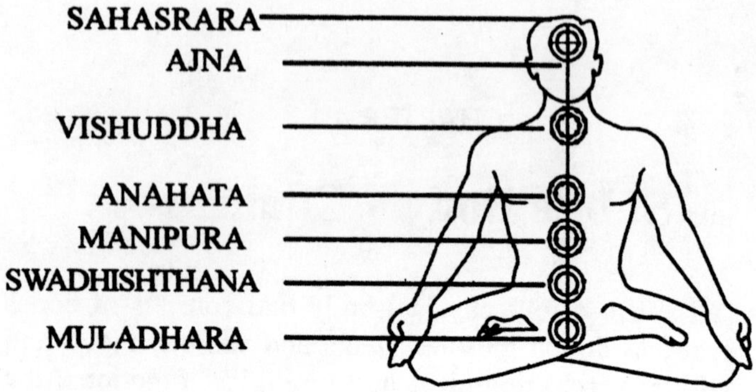

Their corresponding locations in the gross body are respectively

1. Region between rectum and sexual organs
2. Pelvic region
3. Stomach
4. Heart
5. Throat
6. Behind the centre of the eye brows
7. At the top of the Head

The physical body functions through the organs. You have the organs of action, namely the hands, the legs, the mouth, the sexual parts and the excretory parts. These are called the KARMENDRIYAS, that is, organs of action. You also have another set of five, known as the organs of knowledge, the GYANENDRIYAS.

They are the Eyes, the Nose, the Ears, the Tongue and the Skin. Of course, these organs have their external and internal parts and a complicated mechanism that enables them to do whatever is expected of them. However, their PRINCIPLE OF FUNCTION is related to these CHAKRAS in the SUBTLE ENERGY FIELD. For example, you are able to hear with the help of your Ear, which is the external organ for a whole system that enables you to collect the sound waves, convert them into specific type of vibrations, convey the same to the brain where through some electro-chemical process it is registered.

But the concept of SOUND within you is related to the CHAKRA *VISHUDDHA*. This concept is also considered related to the element ETHER.

Long after you have listened to an enthralling music concert you feel the melody is 'still ringing in your ears'. This is an experience all of us have had some time or the other. What does this mean? It means that the experience of the music has transcended the physical level and entered the SUBTLE LEVEL. It exists in the SUBTLE ENERGY FIELD and you are aware of it when your mind is not overwhelmed with some other instant function. The energy Centre connected with this concept of 'sound' in you being the VISHUDDHA CHAKRA, it is this CHAKRA that enables you to have the 'SPIRITUAL EXPERIE-NCE' of music and also enables you if possible to create music. When you talk of a Gifted Musical Genius you are in fact referring to the person whose VISHUDDHA CHAKRA is most powerful.

Similarly each CHAKRA is related to a certain concept. The AJNA CHAKRA is related to your ego, your temperament, your motivations, your emotions and reactions. It may be stated that your physical and Subtle bodies are inseparably linked, like Fire and Heat. Heat is the concomitant energy of fire. Inter linked as they are the Subtle body and the Gross body function as one. To enable you to fully grasp the nature of this subtle body I give a table of the details of the CHAKRAS. If you scrutinise the same you will understand this close link.

THE COLUMNS IN THE CHART OF CHAKRAS

1. Bhuta/Dharma. In this column the elements (Bhuta) and the nature (Dharma) of each Chakra is given.
2. Region: Since the chakras exist only in the Subtle Body which is parallel to the gross body, the corresponding regions in the gross body at which the Chakras are located are given here.
3. In column 3 Sensory-Organs (Gyanendriya) corresponding to each Chakra are given. Buddhi is discrimination. Manas is the recording and memory faculty of the mind. Aham is the 'I' concept. All these three relate to the energy centre AJNA.
4. Organs of action: In this column the organs of action (Karmendriya) related to each Chakra is given.
5. Color: Each Chakra has a color energy dominant or its energy is in harmony with that color energy.

CHART OF CHAKRAS

Chakras	Element Nature *Bhuta Darma*	Location in the body	Sensory organs *Gyana*	Organs of action *Karma*	Colour dominant *Varna*	Air energy *Vayu*	Subtile principle *Tanmatra*	Number of petals *Bindu*	Mono syllable *Bija*
Ajna		Between the eyebrows	Ego mind discrimination	Muscles	Blue - white	Udana		2	Om
Vishuddha	Ether Vacuity	Throat	Ears	Mouth	Transparent	Prana	Sound	16	Ham
Anahata	Air Mobility	Heart	Skin	Hands	Black	Vyana	Touch	12	Yam
Manipura	Fire Luminosity	Stomach	Eyes	Excretion	Red	Samana	Form	10	Ram
Swadhishthana	Water Luquidity	Pelvic	Tongue	Sex	White	Apana	Taste	6	Vam
Muladhara	Earth Solidity	Base	Nose	Legs	Yellow	Apana	Odour	4	Lam

6. Air: In the Yoga Sastra (science of Yoga) it is stated that the air we breathe has subtle energy. This energy entering the body with the air divides itself into five categories. They are *Udana, Prana, Vyana, Sdmana and Apana*. These five categories associate with the Chakras and through their energies are responsible for functions such as use of the voluntary muscles, sensory-organs, circulatory system, sexual and excretory systems. This column shows which Chakra is associated with which air category (Vayu)
7. Tanmatra: This can only be defined as the 'abstract principle'. Sabda is the abstract principle of sound. Sparsa is the abstract principle of touch. Rupa is of form, Rasa of taste and Gandha of odour. Each Chakra is related to the subtle principle of the sense system.
8. Bindu: A point. Units of positive and negative energies that exist in each Chakra. Usually they are shown as the number of petals in a flower.
9. Bija Mantra: The 'monosyllable sound vibration' associated and in harmony with the energy of each Chakra is given here.

COMPARISON OF CHARTS AND SUBTLE ENERGY FIELD

A weak afflicted Subtle Energy Field naturally results in some obstruction or malfunctioning of the physical body. Similarly an afflicted physical body results in the dissipation of the Subtle Energy. Specifically if a certain energy centre, a Chakra is weak, all functions of the organs connected with the energies of that Chakra become debilitated. Any damage to the Subtle Body robs the 'principle' behind the functioning of the corresponding parts of the physical body.

One factor particularly relevant to Comparison that could effect the Subtle Body is the constant close contact with some one whose Subtle Body energies are incompatible with your own. Just as physical bodies differ, the quality and quantum of energy in the various Chakras differ from individual to individual. When two persons are in close contact such as in sexual union in particular, there is mutual interaction of the energies of their Chakras.If there is incompatibility of these Chakras, the constant close contact can effect either or both the persons involved. Incompatible vibrations of the individuals clash and impinge constantly and create disharmony and the Chakra energy is disturbed. In some cases, the person having a weaker Chakra gets affected and in some both may be equally effected.

Once the Chakra energy gets disturbed the corresponding organs of sense and action get effected. The mental and emotional states also get effected. On the other hand where there is harmony in these energies, where there is compatibility of these Chakras, the frequent close contact between the persons, increases the energy levels of the Chakras in one or both the partners.

It is in this context that the concept of the Subtle Body becomes important in Comparison. The Vedic astrological rules for matrimonial harmony take into consideration the harmony of the Subtle Bodies of the couple. Where there is harmony and compatibility in the Subtle Bodies, the couple not only are mentally and emotionally happy but also enjoy a satisfying and invigorating sexual life.

The sages in their wisdom and probably on the basis of statistical testimony, related certain signs, planets and lunar mansions to certain aspects of the Subtle Body and have given rules of comparison to ensure compatibility of the energy centres of the couple. Since the Subtle Body is the spiritual aspect, these rules relate to the spiritual compatibility. I have therefore explained these rules under 'Spiritual Agreement'.

PART III

THE SYSTEM

CHAPTER 5

Lotus of Six Petals

Taking into consideration the various rules regarding comparing of horoscopes and the purpose or object to be realized by applying the rule I have classified them into six categories and call them the six petals of the lotus of astrological comparison.

*1. Comparison of position of Mars.

*2. Comparison of position of Moon.

*3. Comparison of the Nakshatras.

*4. Comparison of the malefic content

*5. Comparison of planetary cycles.

*6. Comparison by planetary mutual positions.

At the outset I should state that it is impossible to find two birth charts that have *all* the required agreements. When you have gone through this book and have understood the methods, you will realize that the very basis of the system *does not aim at securing total agreement.*

The system evolved by me enables one to select a chart that has maximum possible agreement. It also enables one to find the areas of agreement and areas of disagreement so that the couple could work out the methods to overcome the same.

There is a 'down to earth' realistic attitude in the approach of the sages. There can be only large areas of agreement between two individuals that can enable them to live together as husband and wife. The potentiality of the areas of agreement can off set the problems created in the areas of disagreement. In any case, the couple have the right to choose their *priorities* in agreement and disagreement. When the couple knows the possible source of trouble, through proper effort, care and caution they can prevent, overcome or minimize the same.

What do you seek in your matrimonial relationship? Temperamental agreement, emotional equality, enjoyable companionship, psychological support, material support and security, physical satisfaction or spiritual harmony, or all of them? What are your priorities? This system will enable you to know which of these you will have and which you may not have in a particular relationship.

A critical analysis of the rules shows that it was not the intention of the sages to totally condemn a relationship between an intending couple. The aim of the exercise seems to be to discover the positive and negative aspects in each relationship. It is not necessary to pass a judgement on a prospective couple "You are totally unsuitable for each another." The sages seem to say,"Have you realized that if you get married you are likely to run into trouble in these areas of life? Before warned and find the solutions if you want to go ahead. These are the areas of agreement that may help you off set the problems. Take full advantage of them. Decide if it is your cup of tea!"

Before we begin to systematically study each petal in detail, there is one philosophical question which I must answer to set your mind clear regarding the purpose, scope and objectives of this comparison. The question is 'Can the karmic part in ones own life be off set by taking a partner whose chart is most compatible?' The answer is 'NO'.

Your life partner certainly has a karmic relationship with you. It is this karmic relationship that enables you and your partner to share the joy and sorrow of life together, experience the same situations of happiness and suffering. If there is compatibility there can be some amelioration in the experience of negative karma but there will be no elimination of your karma good or bad. So also if there is incompatibility it may enhance the extent of karmic suffering which you have to go through. In other words, your life partner cannot make or break your good or bad karma Compatibility ensures synchronization of karmic experience and therefore such a life partner only enhances the pleasure of good karma and minimizes the suffering of bad karma through sharing and understanding but does not eliminate your karma.

CHAPTER 6

Petal 1

Temperament Agreement/Mars

Mars and Venus are considered planets significant for marriage and married life. While Venus is related to sentiments Mars is related to temperament, Venus to finer feelings and Mars to passions, Venus to agreement and understanding and Mars to combativeness, quarrels and violence. An agreement of Mars is important for the smooth running of marital life. Mars is also the planet connected with separation, break up, divorce and obstructions. It is also connected with the physical urges. The position of Mars in a Horoscope and the comparative position of Mars in both the Horoscopes is important to ensure a stable relationship free from problems.

First we shall consider the position of Mars in an individual's chart and see what it means. We shall consider the position of Mars in the 1st, 2nd, 4th, 7th, 8th, 12th houses only as this position has direct bearing on matrimonial affairs.

Mars in 1st House: This makes the individual aggressive, hot tempered and assertive, dominating and demanding. When Mars is in the first house it has a full aspect on the 7th house, the house of marriage. Hence the 7th is afflicted by Mars and can therefore bring marital problems such as disputes, disagreements, quarrels and even separations. It also aspects the 4th house of domestic happiness and can cause obstructions. It also aspects the 8th house fully. The 8th house is the house of Longevity. Though this does not necessarily mean a short life, it could cause some problems of health. Besides the 8th house happens to be the second house counted from the 7th, which represents the partner. As such it is the house indicating nature of death (MARAKA) of the partner. The aspect of Mars to this house is there-fore not good for the partner.

Mars in the 2nd House: When Mars is in the second house in a chart, its position is not conducive for a happy family life. Being the second it effects the longevity of life partner. Besides its aspect is on the 8th house, which has been discussed. It has an aspect on the 5th house also, which is the house of children and Mars which aspects this house can create some problems in this direction.

Mars in the 4th House: This house is the house of domestic happiness and if Mars is in this house, there is some disturbance. From this position its aspects are on the 7th, 10th, and 11th houses. Its aspects on the 7th, the house of marriage creates problems. The aspects on the 10th and 11th are not relevant for our comparison purpose.

Mars in 7th House: We have already seen that Mars in the 7th house of marriage is not conductive to a happy successful marriage as it can bring friction leading to separation. When Mars is in the 7th house it aspects the 10th which is not relevant for our present discussion. Its aspects to the 1st house and 2nd house are adverse for matrimonial happiness as we have discussed the position of Mars in these houses.

Mars in the 8th House: Mars in this house, which is the house of longevity of the individual concerned and the second from the seventh house indicating the life partner, is not a favorable position. Mars from this house aspects the 11th, not relevant for our discussion., the 1st and 2nd houses, which we have already discussed as unfavorable.

Mars in 12th House: The twelfth house is the house of bed pleasures and the position of Mars in this house can cause obstructions and disruption in sexual pleasure or create excessive, indisciplined indulgence. Also from this position it aspects the 3rd house the house of mental inclination, giving the Individual quick temper and an inclination towards violence. It also aspects the sixth house the house of Health and may bring problems of health that can disturb marital happiness. It also aspects the 7th house, the house of marriage and marital happiness bringing problems in this direction.

KUJA DOSHA—AFFLICTION FROM MARS

From the above considerations it can be seen that comparatively the position of Mars in the 7th, 8th and 12th is most unsuitable than 2nd and 4th. So when we find Mars in any of these places we should realize that there is some latent threat to marital happiness. This Mars affliction is generally termed as MANGAL DOSH in the north of India and KUJA DOSHA OR ANGARAKA DOSHA in South of India. Mangal, Kuja and Angaraka are all names for Mars and Dosha means affliction. Some astrological rules mention exceptions to this affliction. These exceptions are made in a superficial way which are of dubious significance. It is generally considered that if Mars is "well placed", though it is in these houses the affliction does not exist. Being well placed can be: in its own sign, in friendly houses and in a position of exaltation. Which means if Mars is in Aries or Scorpio its own signs, Taurus, Cancer, Leo, Libra, Sagittarius, Aquarius and Pisces which are eight friendly or neutral signs, Capricorn its sign of exaltation, its affliction does not exist. This particularly eliminates ten signs out of the Zodiac of twelve signs and makes consideration of this affliction in Comparison a ludicrous proposition.

My opinion is that it is better to interpret this exception the other way round. Note that Gemini and Virgo do not find a place in the above list.

RULE:

Mars affliction exists in 1st, 2nd, 4th, 7th, 8th and 12th houses; comparatively more if in 1st, 7th, 8th and 12th and much more if anyone of these houses also happens to be in the sign gemini or virgo.

There is another rule mentioned in astrological texts. The position of Mars is to be considered afflicting if in the 1st, 7th, 8th and 12th houses not only counted from the Ascendent, but also from the Moon and also from Venus in the Horoscope. This again apparently is a very dubious rule. For if this rule is applied it would be difficult to find a horoscope without Mars affliction. The best way to apply this rule is to see if Mars happens to be in an adverse sign counted from the Ascendent and consider this affliction *stronger* if it is found in an adverse house counted from Moon and/or Venus also. It is better to basically examine the position of Mars from the Ascendent.

The procedure for deciding Mars affliction is to note the number of sign in which Mars is counting from the Asnd. &/ or Moon &/ or Venus.

1. If in the 2nd and/or 4th from one or more, its affliction is : 30%
2. If in the 1st, 7th, 8th, or 12th from one or more it afflicts: 40%
3. If it is in the 1st, 7th, 8th or 12th from one or more which also happens to be the sign Gemini or Virgo afflicts more: 50%
4. If it is in the 1st, 7th, 8th or 12th not only from Ascendent but also either 1st, 7th, 8th or 12th from Moon or From Venus it afflicts much more: 60%
5. If it is either in 1st, 7th, 8th or 12th from Ascendent, also from Moon and also from Venus it afflicts much more than in 4 : 70%

6. If it is either in 1st, 7th, 8th or 12th from Ascendent, also from Venus and/or Moon and is either in the sign Gemini or Virgo it afflicts most : 80%

These are the six grades of affliction possible, given in the increasing order of affliction. Always start seeing position from Ascendent.

When Mars Affliction may be overlooked !

If Mars is in any of the positions, 1st, 2nd, 4th, 7th, 8th or 12th in a chart there is affliction.

However under a specific circumstances this affliction may be overlooked. I had already explained the calculation of Planetary Cycles. If the person in whose chart there is Mars affliction, is not likely to live through the cycle of Mars after marriage, then this affliction may be ignored as he or she is not likely to experience the adverse results of the affliction generally. The result of Mars affliction is generally experienced during the Planetary Cycle of Mars.

We shall now study the rule in Comparison, the rule to establish compatibility between two charts based on Mars affliction in the charts.

RULE:

Where there is Mars affliction in one Partner's chart, it is advisable that the other partner's chart also has a similar grade affliction,

To explain the rule, it means that if Mars is found in the place of affliction in one chart, it should also be present in the place of affliction in the other chart also. It is also necessary that the level of affliction should be equal. It would be best to have the same level and type.

The principle is that equally afflicted charts are compatible. This is a better way of stating than saying that equally afflicted charts 'Neutralize' the affliction. I do not think that affliction in the chart of one partner can neutralize the affliction in the chart of the other partner. Our aim is to establish compatibility. From this point of view two equally afflicted charts are more compatible.

It is like one handicapped person marrying another handicapped (not necessarily the same type of handicap). Then there will be no complexes interfering with their relationship. Similarly if there is strong Mars affliction in one chart it is obvious there can be a separation or divorce for the person. Because of this planetary position there will be a mental predisposition in anticipating and moving towards such an eventuality. Now if this person married someone whose chart does not have a similar affliction, and therefore a built-in sense of stability and permanence, there are bound to be some problems of approach to marriage and married life. The person with the Mars affliction may act in a way to provoke disharmony, separation leading to divorce. The partner who never dreamed of breaking up is devastated and may enter a period of depression develop feelings of guilt for the failure of the marriage and suffer mentally and emotionally. When there is affliction in both, there is anticipation in both and they may accept the eventuality of a break up as an inevitability. They may even choose to be good friends after such a break. These are the couples who will happily agree to disagree and live together.

Also the basic principle of compatibility implies that both partners should live together as a couple which means there should not be wide differences in their longevity. 'Till death do us part' is the ideal. If there is Mars affliction in one effecting the longevity, then it is certainly advisable to have a partner with similar affliction so that one is not made a widow or widower much earlier in life. (It should be realized that there are many other planetary indications for a short life. It is important to note the study of longevity is a complicated subject and cannot be decided superficially just by the position of Mars.)

Philosophically this rule implies that there is better compatibility when two persons have Karmic equality. My considered opinion is that this Mars affliction being balanced in both the charts should be taken in conjunction with balancing of the Karmic Destiny of both the partners as explained later in Petal number 4.

CHAPTER 7

Petal 2

Moon Sign Agreement Emotional/Psychological

The Moon has a special status in Hindu Astrology. Its importance is understandable being the closest planet to the Earth, a satellite to the earth and as the planet having special influence over ocean tides, agriculture, fecundity and the 'MIND'.

It is the planet connected with human psychology, likes and dislikes, complexes, phobias, depressions, conceptions and convictions. All the positive and negative developments in a person's psychology are related to Moon. As such the comparison of the sign in which Moon is in both the partner's horoscope assumes great significance. Compatibility on this level ensures emotional balance in the relationship. There will be a matching of character and behavior. There will be a proper policy of give and take. The partners will be able to find a satisfactory equation to their relationship. Whatever their individual strengths or failings, they seem to complement and supplement each of their qualities. They fit in like a plug and socket. When there is Moon sign agreement they appear to be made for each other.

THE MOON SIGN AGREEMENT is made in three ways:

(a) On the basis of the Moon signs of the partners.

(b) On the basis of the relationship between the lords of the Moon signs.

(c) On the basis of a special classification of signs known as VASHYA.

We shall consider them one by one.

A. RASHI AGREEMENT

RULE: **Rule on the basis of the Moon Signs of the Partners**

Note the sign in which Moon is in both the charts. Count from the Female Moon sign. If from Female Moon Sign, the Male Moon Sign is the 7th it is best, if 8th, 9th, 10th, 11th or 12th it is good, but if it is 2nd, 3rd, 4th, 5th or 6th it is not good for a compatible relationship. If both are same sign their nakshatras should differ for compatibility.

EXAMPLE: If the Female Moon Sign is Scorpio and the Male Sign is Leo, counting from the Female Moon Sign the Male Moon Sign is in the 10th. Hence there is Moon Sign compatibility.

Critical Study:

From the rule it is seen the best position the partners can have is to have the Moons in Opposite signs. As already mentioned the principle is to ensure that the qualities of the partners are both complimentary and supplementary. Astrologically the opposite signs are both complimentary and supplementary. The following table gives the relationship

RELATED SIGNS		RULERS	RELATIONSHIP	
ARIES ...	LIBRA	Mars/Venus	Mundane...	Sublime
SCORPIO...	TAURUS	Mars/Venus	Passions...	Sentiments
GEMINI...	SAGIT	Mercury/Jupiter	Knowledge..	Wisdom
VIRGO...	PISCES	Mercury/Jupiter	Learning...	Intuition
CANCER...	CAPRI	Moon/Saturn	Flexibility...	Fixity
LEO...	AQUAR	Sun/Saturn	Expansion...	Equilibrium

When Moons are in opposite signs there is a strong mutual aspect between the Moons, which means a strong "meeting of minds" each being the natural partner for the other.

When the time of birth is not know the Ascendent cannot be calculated. In such cases generally in the west, the Sun sign is taken as the ascendent. In Hindu Astrology in such cases the Moon sign is taken as the Ascendent.

In a chart let us consider the Moon sign as the Ascendent or rising sign. The following figure gives the position of Moon sign. as rising sign.

RASHI

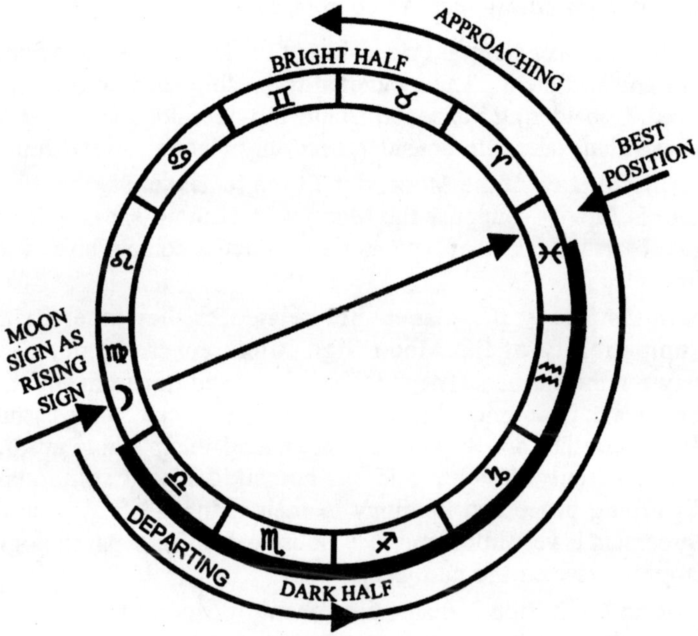

From the figure it can be seen that the signs 2 to 6 are in the DARK HALF as they are signs yet to rise in the eastern horizon. Signs 8 to 12 are in the bright half. If the partner's MOON SIGN is in signs 2 to 6 it is considered not good and if from 8 to 12 good. The figure fully explains the logic in the rule.

Further it can be seen from the figure, if the Partner's Moon is between 2nd and 6th signs it means the partner's Moon is moving away from her Moon, whereas if it is between the 8th and 12th signs it means his Moon is approaching her Moon and naturally this later relation between the Moons is better than the former.

B. RASHI LORDS

Comparison of the relationship of the rulers of the Moon Signs

RULE:

Note the ruler of the Female Moon sign. The ruler of the Moon Sign of the Male should be a friend. If so there is compatibility. If it is neutral there is average compatibility. If it is an enemy there is no compatibility.

Here we take Natural Friendship of the Planets. This is necessary and sufficient. The incidental friendship need not be considered. Considering incidental friendship does not appear logical. So we shall take into consideration only Natural Friendship.

EXAMPLE: If the Moon sign of the female is Sagittarius, its ruler is Jupiter. Suppose the Moon sign of the Male is Aries, its ruler Mars is a friend of Jupiter. Hence there is compatibility under this rule.

In Astrology the planets are related to the 'inner being'. Compatibility of the Moon Sign rulers ensures inner peace between the partners. They will be related and free from any inner tensions in their union. Inner tensions experienced by the partners living together are responsible for several inexplicable attitudes that gradually develop and surface suddenly at some stage, disturbing peace and harmony in their married life. Hence this agreement is very important to establish a deep inner psychological rapport between the partners.

Rule I and Rule 2 ensure agreement of Moon Sign and Moon sign rulers, which means ensuring compatibility of behavioral psychology as well as subconscious patterns. As such the Moon Sign agreement constitutes the most important agreement in Hindu astrological comparison. The emotional and psychological aspects of compatibility are covered here.

Before I go to the third method of comparison by Moon sign, I would like to present a ready reference table which combines these two rules, under Moon Sign Agreement. This will help to logically assess the relationship and grade it on the basis of rules A & B.. I will explain how I have prepared it.

1. The first rule says that the Moon Sign of the male if 7th from the Moon Sign of the female is 'best', if between 8th and 12th 'good' and if between 2nd and 6th 'not good'.

2. The second rule says if the ruler of the Male Moon sign is a friend of the Female Moon sign it is best, if neutral it is good and if enemy it is not good.

Combining these two rules it can be seen 9 types of combinations are possible and the relationship could also be graded. The type of gradation used in preparing the table is as follows:

1. For Friendly Relationship I use 'F' = 100.
2. For Neutral Relationship I use 'N' = 50.
3. For Inimical Relationship I use 'E' = 0.

For sign position I give

7th house = 100 Best

8th to 12th house = 50 Good

2nd to 6th house = 0 Not Good

Case 1 : Male Moon Sign in 7th from Female Moon Sign-BEST

Ruler if Friend ...100+100 = 200 ...F1 (friend-grade 1)
Ruler if Neutral ... 50+100 = 150 ...N2 (neutral-grade2)
Ruler if Enemy ... 0+100 = 100 ...E3 (enemy-grade 3)

Case 2 : Male Moon Sign is between 8th and 12th Sign-GOOD

Ruler is Friend ...100+50 = 150 ...F2 (friend-grade 2)
Ruler is Neutral ... 50+50 = 100 ...N3(neutral-grade 3)
Ruler is Enemy ... 0+ 0 = 50 ...E4 (enemy-grade 4)

Case 3 : Male Moon Sign is between 2nd and 6th Sign - NOT-GOOD

Ruler is Friend ...100+0 = 100 ...F3 (friend-grade 3)
Ruler is Neutral ... 50+0 = 50 ...N4(neutral-grade 4)
Ruler is Enemy ... 0+0 = 0 ...E5 (enemy-grade 5)

This is the order of compatibility. The best compatibility based on both rules is F1, and the least compatible is E5. We can consider these nine grades of agreement at three levels based on units strength.

The best agreement grades	F1, N2, F2.	(200,150)
The average agreement grades	E3, N3, F3.	(100)
The least agreeable grades	E4, N4, E5.	(50, 0)

In the following Table on the left vertical column you have the sign of the female. Look up the Male Moon Sign on the top horizontal. Find the corresponding relationship and you have the level of agreement based on the two rules at once.

MALE

FEMALE

Signs & Rulers	♈	♉	♊	♋	♌	♍	♎	♏	♐	♑	♒	♓
♈		**N4**	**E5**	F3	F3	**E5**	N2	F2	F2	N3	N3	F2
♉	N3		F3	**E5**	**E5**	F3	F3	N2	N3	F2	F2	N3
♊	N3	F2		**E5**	F3	F3	F3	**N4**	N2	N3	N3	N3
♋	N3	F2	F2		F3	F3	F3	**N4**	**N4**	N4	N3	N3
♌	F2	E4	N3	F2		N4	**E5**	F3	F3	**E5**	E3	F2
♍	N3	F2	F2	E4	F2		F3	**N4**	**N4**	**N4**	**N4**	N2
♎	N2	F2	F2	E4	E4	F2		**N4**	**N4**	F3	F3	N4
♏	F3	N2	E4	F2	F2	E4	N3		F3	**N4**	**N4**	F3
♐	F3	**E5**	E3	F2	F2	E4	E4	F2		**N4**	**N4**	F3
♑	**E5**	F3	F3	F3	**E4**	F2	F2	E4	N3		F3	**N4**
♒	**E5**	F3	F3	**E5**	E3	F2	F2	E4	N3	F2		**N4**
♓	F3	**E5**	**E5**	F3	F3	E3	E4	F2	F2	N3	N3	

I would like to call your attention to the fact that the most ideal according to both the rules, that is **F1** ***does not exist at all.*** *How very particularly true!!* Therefore N2 and F2 are the best possible.

In case you find that the relationship between the Male Moon sign and Female Moon sign is the last category that is E4, N4 or E5 it means there is a wide psychological gap between the partners. They should hasten to rectify the problem by identifying the zones of friction in their psychology before it is too late.

Though the table enables you to readily see the level of the Moon Sign agreement it is advisable to individually check up the Sign agreement and the agreement of the rulers the Moon Signs, so that you will know where the source of trouble lies, whether in the external behavior pattern and outward characteristics (Sign disagreement) or in some deep inner fears or complexes or fixations (rulers disagreement).

Before I conclude the discussion on this rule I would like to give a list of indications given in some Hindu Astrological classics regarding the results of the different placements of the Moon signs of the couple.

These interesting results are as follows:

If the Male Moon Sign counted from the Female Moon Sign

is in the 12th ..... Gives good longevity for the relationship.

is in the 11th ..... Gives happiness and gain for the couple.

is in the 10th ..... Gives mutual affection.

is in the 9th ..... Gives mutual loyalty.

is in the 8th ..... Gives increased responsibility for the couple.

is in the 7th ..... Gives a lot of success and happiness.

is in the 6th ..... Brings loss or trouble through children.

is in the 5th ..... Obstructs material support to the wife from the husband.

is in the 4th ..... Brings inimical attitudes and quarrels.

is in the 3rd ..... Brings frequent unhappy events.

is in the 2nd ..... Obstructs the pleasure of companionship .... particularly for the male.

You will note that the nature of readings are generally in agreement with the rule A given about signs. The dominant issue of agreement or disagreement in each case is given in the above readings.

C. ON THE BASIS OF VASHYA :

Special Classification of Signs

Literally VASHYA means 'under control' or 'attraction' The zodiac signs are allotted to two groups. There are some slight differences in different classical texts and some of the alternatives found are given in the brackets.

GROUP 1.	GROUP 2	SIGN NO. COUNTED FROM GROUP 1
Aries	Leo, Scorpio	5th and 8th
Taurus	Cancer & Libra (Leo)	3rd and 6th (4)
Gemini	Virgo	4th
Cancer	Scorpio, Sagittarius	5th and 6th
Leo	Libra	3rd
Virgo	Pisces, Gemini	7th and 10th
Libra	Capricorn (Virgo)	4th and (12th)
Scorpio	Cancer	9th
Sagittarius	Pisces	4th
Capricorn	Aries, Aquarius	4th and 2nd
Aquarius	Virgo (Aries)	8th and (3rd)
Pisces	Aries (Capricorn)	2nd and (11th)

RULE:

The rule is that the Male Moon Sign should be in Group 2 corresponding to the Female Moon Sign in Group 1.

Note the Female Moon sign in Group 1. See the Moon sign or signs indicated for it in Group 2. If the Male Moon sign belongs to this there is agreement under Vasya.

This agreement ensures much cooperation between the partners. There will be a 'give and take' attitude, a desire to be cooperative and obliging. We have seen that under Moon Sign agreement Rule 1, it was considered best if the Male Moon sign was 7th from that of the Female, good if from 8th to 12th not good if from 2 to 6.

However if you study the above list where I have given the number of the Moon sign of the male from that of the female you will note that they are all between 2 and 7 except a few. The idea obviously is that while rule 1, generally says it is best for the female to choose a man whose Moon sign is anywhere between 7 and 12, this rule tells which among those between 2 and 6 would also be suitable, so that the disagreeable signs are minimized.

Critical Study:

The careful selection of the compatible signs within 2 and 6 has been made bearing in mind that the stability or permanence in a union can be ensured, if one of the partners is dominant and the other submissive. We have seen that the sages gave importance to the Female, as in the whole comparison system there is an implied concept that matrimonial stability is more or less a certainty where the female has the last word, where the lady is the light of the house. It is on the basis of these fundamental concepts that the agreeable signs have been chosen, specifically to offset the adverse effects indicated under 'interesting results' at the end of rules1 and 2. In discussing the logic of the signs allotted in group 2, I shall not deal in the regular order from Aries to Pisces, but only with the allotment of the male moon sign from female moon sign between 2 and 6.

MALE MOON SIGN 2nd FROM FEMALE MOON SIGN:

It has been indicated that in such a case the result is 'Lack of company of wife' it means that for some reason the husband is denied the company of the wife, often or periodically due to circumstances beyond control. Under these circumstances, if the union is to survive, the male has to fill the time through other activities in which he can partake with great enthusiasm. That is why for a Piscean Female an Arien husband and for a Capricorn Female an Aquarian male have been suggested in the Vashya list.

MALE MOON SIGN IS 3rd FROM FEMALE MOON SIGN:

In such a situation the result is 'frequent unhappy events'. In the Vashya grouping the Taurus Female is given the Cancer male which is the third sign from Taurus. The female with Moon in Taurus is gifted with determination and the capacity to resist outside influences. She is conservative, intuitive and has good judgement and can certainly help the home-loving changeable Cancer male who is susceptible to outside influences and thus avoid the unhappy events, or help face them with equanimity.

MALE MOON SIGN IS 4th FROM FEMALE MOON SIGN:

The result given is 'inimical attitudes and quarrels'. To overcome this the best choice is to allot the Virgo male to the Gemini female. Both being ruled by Mercury, this would minimize inimical attitudes and quarrels that could arise out of inner psychological strains.

MALE MOON SIGN IS 5th FROM FEMALE MOON SIGN:

The result given is 'lack of material support to the wife from the husband'. In this category we find in the Vashya list Leo Male permitted for the Arian Female and the Scorpio Male allotted to the Cancer Female. The males with Moon in Leo and Scorpio would be the last persons not to provide material support to their partners as it is part of their egoistic satisfaction to provide the material support, even if the support is not given out of love or a sense of duty. This is the case of the Aries and Cancer Female where the sages were able to pick out a 5th sign agreeable male partners.

MALE MOON SIGN IS 6th FROM FEMALE MOON SIGN:

The result given is 'loss or trouble through children'. Under these circumstances the female has to be a home-loving person with great endurance and fortitude, and one much more articulate than the male in bringing up the children. This is certainly the Cancer mother. The 6th sign would be Sagittarius.The Moon in Sagittarius male would be kind hearted, good humored, easily forgiving, hopeful and fond of children. Therefore, this is certainly the best combination to overcome the problems that would arise when the male Moon sign is 6th from the female.

I have briefly discussed the merits of the grouping in Vashya to show how carefully the sages tried to prepare a permissible list of agreeable Moon signs out of those which are totally prohibited under rule 1 of Moon sign agreement.

Taking rules A & C it is clear that in most cases there can be only one, either Rashi Agreement or Vashya Agreement. In only a few cases there can be both. (See table at the end of the book)

CHAPTER 8

Petal 3

Nakshatra Agreements

A. VEDHA/OBSTRUCTIONS

Literally VEDHA means to pierce, to obstruct. It indicates the worry that comes out of prejudiced attitudes between the partners. Life would be torturous on account of such an incompatibility. A list of Nakshatras and the corresponding Nakshatras which are having Vedha - opposition to them are given. The list is as follows:

Nakshatra No.	Name of the Nakshatra	Opposed to Nakshatra No.	Name of the Nakshatra
1.	Ashwini	18	Jyeshtha
2.	Bharani	17	Anuradha
3.	Krittika	16	Vishakha
4.	Rohini	15	Swati
5.	Mrigashira	14, 23	Chitra, Dhanishtha
6.	Ardra	22	Shravana
7.	Punarvasu	21	Uttara Ashadha
8.	Pushya	20	Purva Ashadha
9.	Ashlesha	19	Moola
10.	Magha	27	Revati
11.	Poorva Phalguni	26	Uttara Bhadrapada
12.	Uttara Phalguni	25	Poorva Bhadrapada
13.	Hasta	24	Shatabhisha

RULE:

The Nakshatras of the couple should not be the opponents as per the above table.

EXAMPLE: If the Female Nakshatra is Pushya the 8th Nakshatra, the Male Nakshatra should not be the 20th Purva Ashadha or if for example the male Nakshatra is Mrigashira the 5th the female should not be either Chitra the 14th or Dhanishtha the 23rd or if the female is Revati the 27th, the male should not be the 10th Nakshatra, Magha.

The thrust of this agreement is that if they belong to the opposing Nakshatras they will be an unlucky pair. One will prove obstructive and unlucky to the other. Who will prove unlucky to whom, whether male or female is a different matter, which depends on the individual charts. That is not the issue of study here. If one partner is found to be causing obstructions and bad luck to the other, sooner or later the other is sure to discover this aspect in their relationship. There could be nothing more discouraging for the continuation of the relationship, than such a discovery. A hatred, dislike and prejudice is formed.

This comparison is of importance for the material welfare as well as psychological compatibility of the partners. The psychological aspect is also significant as one partner may be unconsciously doing things that can create failure and setbacks in the affairs of the other partner and this may be construed as 'ill-luck' brought over by the partner.

We have all had the experience of hearing statements between such ill matched couples, statements such as :

- You are always unlucky for me.
- Any work of mine entrusted to you gets ruined.
- You always create problems in my way.
- Nothing works when we both go together anywhere.
- I lose my balance and confidence in your presence.

These are some of the typical statements made by one of the partners to the other, when he or she feels there is some ill luck being created by the other. To avoid such a situation in married life Vedic synastry suggests avoiding disagreement of Nakshatras as per the list given.

Critical Study: Let as examine the logic in this grouping. The following figure shows the twelve Zodiac signs and the 27 Nakshatra divisions.

VEDHA NAKSHATRAS

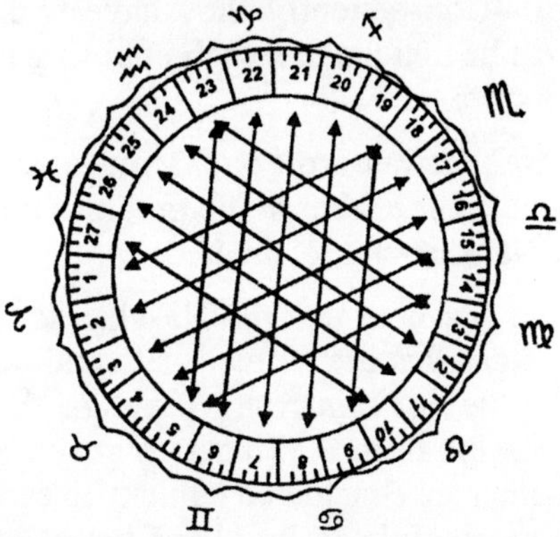

NAK. NO.	SIGN	OPP. TO	SIGN	MUTUAL POSITION
1 2	♈	18 17	♏	8~6
3 4	♉	16 15	♎	6~8
6 7	♊	22 21	♑	8~6

NAK. NO.	SIGN	OPP. TO	SIGN	MUTUAL POSITION
8 9	♋	20 19	♐	6~8
10 11	♌	27 26	♓	8~6
12 13	♍	25 24	♒	6~8

IT CAN BE READILY SEEN THAT SPLIT NAKSHATRAS NOS. 5, 14, 23 ARE OPPOSED TO EACH OTHER

The principle behind the listing of the Nakshatras and their opponents can be well understood by a study of the figure. The figure shows the Nakshatras in the Zodiac and the arrow shows its opponents. There are three sets here:

1. Nakshatras 1 to 5 have Nakshatras 14 to 18 opposed in the reverse order.
2. Nakshatras 6 to 9 have Nakshatras 19 to 23 opposed in the reverse order.
3. Nakshatras 10 to 14 have Nakshatras 23 to 27 opposed in the reverse order.

Besides you can also observe from the figure Nakshatras 5, 14, 23 having two Nakshatras in opposition to each. These three are Nakshatras, Mrigashira, Chitra, Dhanishtha which are Nakshatras that are equally split between two Zodiac signs and do not fall in one single sign. Consequently they have two Nakshatras in opposition. It will be noticed that each opposing Nakshatra is not 180 degrees opposite.

Why those Nakshatras are considered obstructive will be understood if you see the table in the previous page giving signs in which those Nakshatras are situated.

From the table you note that the Nakshatras opposed to each other belong to signs that are mutually 8th and 6th to each other. If planet B is in the 6th sign from planet A, then A will automatically be in the 8th from B. Planets, signs or houses mutually 8 and 6 to each other are considered unlucky to each other in Vedic Astrology. This principle is involved here. Partners born in Nakshatras which belong to zodiac signs that are mutually 6 and 8 to each other cannot prove to be lucky. As a couple they are likely to create obstructions and bad luck to one another.

B. DINA/TEMPERAMENTAL

DINA literally means 'DAY'. It may have been so named because this agreement ensures mental harmony in the daily activities of the couple. There will be smooth sailing in most of the day to day activities.The mental states of the couple will be complementary to each other with the result that each will act as a balancing force on the other resulting in well balanced decisions and successful programming that makes each day better.

RULE:

The rule is to Count from the female Nakshatra to the male Nakshatra taking both into account. If this number is 9 or more, divide it by 9 and the remainder is the required number.

(a) *If the required number is even, that is 0, 2, 4, 6 or 8 there is agreement under this category*

(b) *If the required number is 3, 5, 7 then there is no agreement.*

(c) *If the required number is 1, which means both belong to the same Nakshatra or Nakshatras having same planetary rulers, then (i) if they belong to the same Moon Sign or Nakshatras having same planetary rulers there is no agreement, and (ii) if they belong to same*

Nakshatras but different Moon Signs there is agreement. (This is possible only for Nakshatras 3, 5, 7, 12. 14, 16, 21, 23, 25 which extend over two signs)

EXAMPLE: A.Female Nakshatra Shatabhisha (24th) -Male Nakshatra Punarvasu (7th). Counting from Shatabhisha as 1, we find Punarvasu is the 11th. Dividing this number by 9, we get the remainder is 2; Hence there is agreement.

EXAMPLE: B. Female Nakshatra is Pushya (8th) and Male Nakshatra is Uttara Phalguni (12th). The required number is 5. Hence there is no agreement.

EXAMPLE: C. If both Female and Male Nakshatras are Krittika there is agreement only if one of them is in the First Pada or quarter of Krittika and other is in any of the other Padas, in which case one will have Moon in Aries and the other in Taurus.

Critical Study: Though the rule has been presented in the mathematical method, the basic principle behind this seemingly arbitrary process of calculation is very simple. Just as the signs in the Zodiac are alternately considered positive and Negative starting with Aries (Mesham) so also the Nakshatras are considered positive and negative alternately. The Nakshatras are divided into three groups of 9 each. The Nakshatras are marked positive and negative alternately. See the diagram.

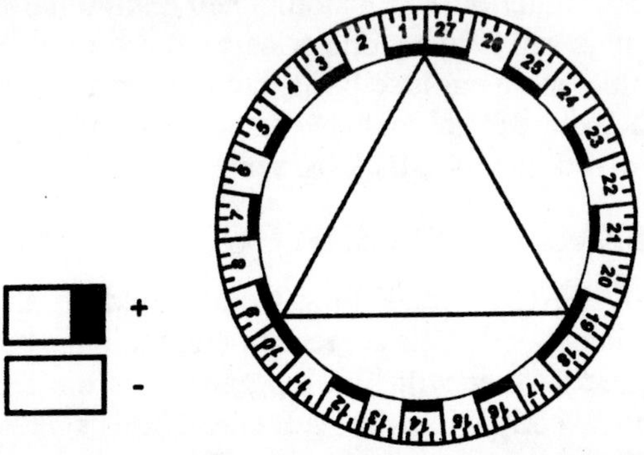

Move the vertex of the triangle to the Nakshatra of the girl to know all agreeable Nakshatras. If the girls Nakshatra is 1(+), it can be seen that the 2nd, 4th, 6th, 8th, 11th, 13th etc. from it are naturally complimentary (-) in nature whereas 3,5,7,9 etc. are the same (+). The principle seems to be that one should belong to positive and another to negative Nakshatras so that there will be a balance.

It is the same principle of positive and negative involved when we are told that if both belong to the same Nakshatra they should belong to different padas such that their Moon signs are different. For example, if both belong to MRIGASHIRA, the 5th Nakshatra and if one belongs to the first half of the Nakshatra, the Moon Sign is Taurus and the one who belongs to the second half has Moon Sign Gemini. Though both belong to the same Nakshatra, the positive-negative relationship is established by sign, as the Zodiac Taurus belongs to the negative group and Gemini to the positive group.

This rule sees to it, that the partners belong to different terminals one to positive and the other to negative. This ensures that the moods are balanced. If one is in a pessimistic mood on a day the other will be in an optimistic mood and give sufficient encouragement or if one is in a state of excessive enthusiasm the other can moderate the situation to avoid the dangers of over enthusiasm. Thus the partners will be able to moderate each other in their day today activities and decisions.

Since DINA means the day and the day implies the Sun that represents the ego, this Nakshatra agreement ensures that there is no 'clash of egos' between the partners. The combination of the positive and negative ensures the evolving of a common ego for the couple and they function in unision. Their individual egos blend perfectly. It is only when one tries to force one's own decision and opinion on an egoistic basis that problems arise and this is avoided when there is union between positive and negative Nakshatras as evolved in this DINA agreement.

C. STREE DEERGA / PSYCHOLOGICAL

Literally *STREE DEERGA* means 'long womanhood'. It simply implies 'delayed widowhood'. This agreement present in the couple means that the male partner will live long and thus the female partner will not suffer early widowhood. Basically this agreement ensures a long married life and companionship. Widow remarriages were a rarity in ancient India and hence a long living marital partner was the ideal sought by the female. It may be asked if the male of the species did not aim at the same thing and wanted a long living wife. Certainly it was the ideal situation sought by the male partner as well. (See blessings of the priest in page IX) However, Vedic Astrology gives the female the prerogative. All rules take the female chart as standard and then compare the male chart to ensure success and happiness in married life. The rule is stated from the female point of view. Besides a 'long married life' sought by a female is dependent on her own longevity. The main idea seems to be that one partner does not survive the other for many long lonely years. Since the female chart endows her with a certain longevity, the aim is to secure a partner who will live long enough or comparatively longer than her own longevity giving her a life time of happy companionship.

This is a concept that holds good in any country and at any period since no female who enjoys the companionship, love and affection from an ideally matched partner would like that their relationship to be cut short by the early demise of the partner.

Rule: *Count from Female Nakshatra to Male Nakshatra both inclusive. If the value is 15 or more there is full agreement under this category. If the value is between 8 and 14 there is average agreement. If it is between 1 and 7 there is no agreement.*

EXAMPLE: If the female Nakshatra is Pushya, the 8th Nakshatra and the Male Nakshatra is Magha the 10th, counting from the Female Nakshatra the Male Nakshatra is the 3rd and hence there is no agreement. If the Male Nakshatra is Anuradha the 17th Nakshatra, counting from the female it would be the 10th. Hence there would be average agreement. If the Male Nakshatra is Dhanishtha the 23rd, counting from the 8th, the Female Nakshatra the Male Nakshatra is the 16th. Hence there is agreement.

Critical Study: This rule seems to have been evolved according to the principle of visible half and invisible half of the Zodiac.

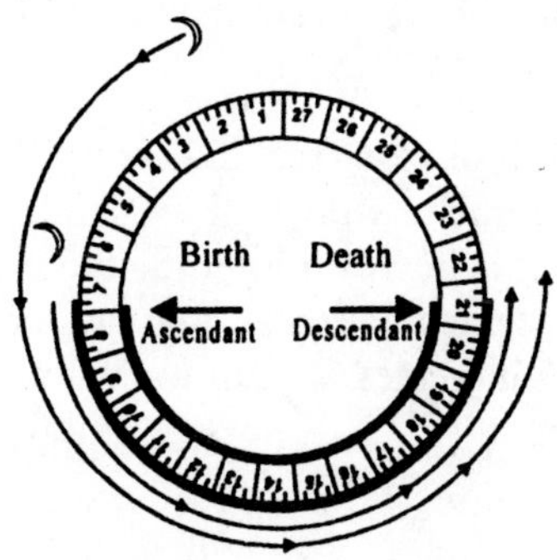

If the moon sign of the female is considered the rising sign, that is the sign on the eastern horizon (as already seen under Moon sign agreement) starting from mid point of the female Nakshatra, the 2nd, the 3rd Nakshatra after it, which have yet to rise are all in the dark half, up to the 14th Nakshatra. This is a longitude of about 180^0 since 14 Nakshatras each of 13^0 20' will equal to 186°-40'. The end of the 14th Nakshatra is exactly on the western horizon. Thereafter, all Nakshatras are in the visible bright half, that is Nakshatras which have already risen.

If you study the illustration you will note that the Female Nakshatra is marked on the eastern horizon as though it were the ascendant. The mid point of the Nakshatra is taken as the rising point on the horizon, the ascendant. The end of the 14th Nakshatra therefore falls on setting point on the opposite horizon. That is why the rule states that the Male Nakshatra should be the 15th or more from the female Nakshatra.

Let us presume that the male Nakshatra is the 2nd and the Female Nakshatra is the 7th. Counting from the Female Nakshatra the male Nakshatra is 23 Nakshatras away. The setting point for the female would be the end of the 14th Nakshatra from the 7th, that is the 20th Nakshatra. The male Moon in the 2nd Nakshatra takes longer to reach this setting point than the female Moon which is in the 7th Nakshatra. Since longevity in Vedic Astrology is calculated by the Dasha system on the basis of the Moons position here we find that the Male Moon reaches the 'setting point' later than the female. Since synchronizing of planetary configuration is the basis of astrology, this symbolically means the male would survive the female. Assured of the happiest union, the ideal of the Hindu woman was to breath the last in the tender embrace of her beloved.

Critical Study: It is obvious that if there is RASHI AGREEMENT (Moon sign agreement: rule 1) there is also STREE DEERGA AGREEMENT. It is however important to note that the existence of this agreement does not mean that the female will predecease the male. It only indicates an astrological probability of a longer life for the male.

D. MAHENDRA/MATERIAL

Mahendra is the king of the gods according to Hindu Mythology. Mahendra therefore symbolically refers to material wealth, prosperity, comforts and the luxuries of life.

RULE: *Count from Female Nakshatra to Male Nakshatra both inclusive. If the value is either 4, 7, 10, 13, 16, 19, 22 or 25 there is full Mahendra agreement.*

When there is this agreement the couple will enjoy good wealth, material comfort and luxuries. They will enjoy economic security, physical comforts and the home environment will be contented. The couple, through their careers or other sources of income, will be successful in fulfilling the financial obligations which go with marital life. This agreement ensures that there would not be friction in the married life on account of financial insecurity of one of the partners. Sometimes there is a feeling in one of the partners that the other is not contributing to the family resources adequately and consequently the family is denied certain essentials. Economic factors are responsible for a lot of marital friction and this agreement ensures that such a situation does not arise. For example, if the Female Nakshatra is *Sravana,* the 22nd and the Male Nakshatra is *Rohini* the 4th Nakshatra, counting from the Female Nakshatra the Male Nakshatra is the 10th. Hence there is Mahendra agreement.

Critical Study: The fourth house in a birth chart is consi-dered the house related to comforts, material prosperity, luxuries & acquisition of property, lands and other assets. Most of the material matters are judged from the fourth house. This principle seems to have been used in evolving this rule, as the numbers given represent every fourth Nakshatra, starting from the Female Nakshatra.

There is another significant point. From any Nakshatra taking every fourth to form one set of agreeable Nakshatras under this category we obviously get 3 groups of 9 Nakshatras. The Nakshatras of the couple may belong to any one group for agreement. You will notice that one group of Nakshatras are ruled by Sun, Mercury and Rahu. The second group is ruled by Moon, Jupiter and Ketu. The third group is ruled by Saturn, Mars and Venus. You can start the count from any Nakshatra.

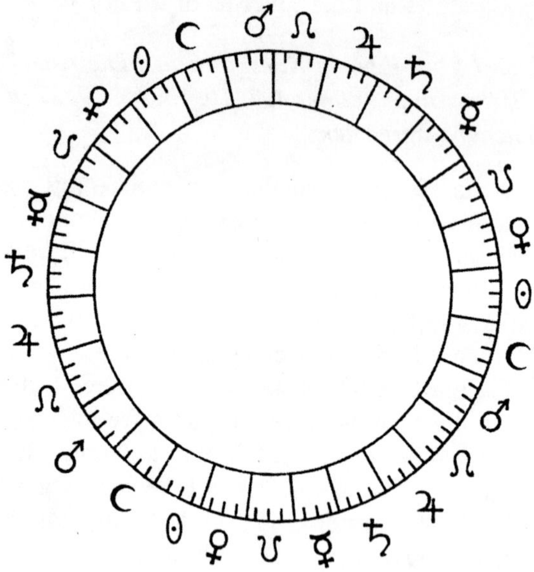

G 1 ... Sun, Rahu, Mercury – Related to FORCE / ACTION

G 2 ... Moon, Ketu, Jupiter – Related to CREATIVITY / ETHICS

G 3 ... Mars, Venus, Saturn – Related to EMOTIVE / REACTION

Though every fourth Nakshatra has been taken to form a group, it is seen that there is a logic in the planetary set lordships of these groups. If both partners belong to the same group, their attitudes towards planning, acquiring, saving and building up material prosperity would be complimentary and not contradictory.

The luminaries Sun and Moon lead two groups while Saturn leads the third. The remaining three malefic planets Rahu, Ketu and Mars go one to each group. The three remaining benefic planets go one to each. Mercury goes to the Sun group, Jupiter to the Moon group and Venus to the Saturn group a logical allocation based on planetary friendships.

Another logic of this grouping can be seen if the padas of the Nakshatras are studied. You will notice that the first Nakshatra Ashwini (1st) ruled by Ketu has four padas allotted to set Aries, Taurus, Gemini and Cancer. Similarly the Nakshatra ruled by Moon Rohini (4th) and the Nakshatra Punarvasu (7th) ruled by Jupiter have the same padas allotted. Thus we find the three Nakshatras ruled by Ketu, Moon and Jupiter have the same pada sub division and therefore belong to a category. Similarly, the Nakshatras ruled by Saturn, Mars and Venus have the same pada sub divisions and belong to one category. Also the three Nakshatras ruled by Sun, Rahu and Mercury have the same pada sub division to form one category. The logic in this grouping is apparent.

The 'fourth' place from the ascendant sign is the place of material acquisitions. This principle is extended to Nakshatras as well and this extension is supported on account of the harmony in the planetary lordships of the Nakshatra groups and their pada lordships also.

Special Notes: For example, if the Female Nakshatra is *Bharani* (2nd) and the Male Nakshatra is *Pushya* (8th) the Male Nakshatra being 7th from the Female Nakshatra rules out *DINA* agreement. So also we find that other combinations that have Mahendra agreement cannot have *DINA* agreement. By now it is clear that it is not possible to find two birth charts having all the agreements. It is also very difficult to find two birth charts in total disagreement. The rules seem to aim at the possibility of alternative agreements. If you do not find agreement on one basis there is a possibility of agreement existing on another basis. The question then is of individual priorities and choices, which agreements *you* prefer.

E. YONI/PHYSICAL

Yoni means the Female sexual organ. This agreement ensures that the male is sexually compatible to the female. This synastry rule helps to ensure that there is no problem on account of sexual dissatisfaction and incompatibility.

To make the application of the rule easy, the sages have allotted an animal to each of the 27 Nakshatras. I give below the list:

Nakshatra	Animal	Nakshatra	Animal
1	Male Horse	15	Male Buffalo
2	Male Elephant	16	Female Tiger
3	Female Sheep	17	Female Deer
4	Male Snake	18	Male Deer
5	Female Snake	19	Female Dog
6	Male Dog	20	Male Monkey
7	Female Cat	21	Mangoose
8	Male Sheep	22	Female Monkey
9	Male Cat	23	Female Lion
10	Male Rat	24	Female Horse
11	Female Rat	25	Male Lion
12	Male Bull	26	Female cow
13	Female Heifer	27	Female Elephant
14	Male Tiger		

In the above list the animals that are mutual enemies are:

Monkey x Sheep
Dog x Deer
Rat x Cat
Horse x Buffalo
Cow x Tiger
Lion x Elephant
Serpent x Mangoose

RULE:

There is full compatibility when the couple belong to the same animal male and female category. Ideal if the male belongs to the male animal and the female belongs to the female of the same species. However as long as both belong to the same animal the reversal of sex is not of importance.

The second category permissible is when the couple belong to friendly animals of the same sex or opposite sex.

The last category which is not compatible is when the couple belong to mutually inimical animals.

Comments:

Sage *VATSYAYANA* who wrote an elaborate treatise *KAMA-SUTRA* on love and sex described the sexual requirements, urges and instincts of man and woman using a comparison with certain animals. In astrology also, based on the characteristic attributes of the Nakshatras each Nakshatra has been related to a certain animal. However for our purpose it is not important to know why a certain animal has been allotted to a certain Nakshatra.The allotment has been made only to make the sexual compatibility test easy. There is an immediate mental acceptance or rejection in connection with sexual harmony once we note the animals to which the couple belong based on their Nakshatras.

Without going into the details of the logic of this allocation let us tabulate the ideal combinations based on the animal relationships.

IDEAL COMBINATIONS:

First we shall group the Nakshatras of the same animals so that we have the Table of ideal combinations. I use Nakshatra numbers only. The specific pairs are :

1	and	24	4	and	5
2	and	27	6	and	19
3	and	8	7	and	9
10	and	11	14	and	16
12	and	26	17	and	18
13	and	15	20	and	22
23	and	25			

In the above Table if the male and female belong to any particular combination there is the possibility of complete physical compatibility and conjugal satisfaction in the married life. (See ready reckoner table at the end of the book.)

INCOMPATIBLE COMBINATIONS:

In the above Table we have the compatible pairs of Nakshatras. If one of Nakshatras in the pair is incompatible with another Nakshatra, naturally the other Nakshatra in the pair will also be compatible with that Nakshatra and its compatible pair. So in the following table you will find pairs of compatible Nakshatras opposed to another pair of compatible Nakshatras.

1, 24	×	13, 15	4, 5	×	21
2, 27	×	23, 25	6, 19	×	17, 18
3, 8	×	20, 22	7, 9	×	10, 11
12, 26	×	14, 16			

It is possible that a couple could belong to Nakshatras that do not find a place in either of these Tables. They may be considered as average and acceptable. If both male and female belong to Nakshatras on the same side of X then certainly, it is acceptable though not ideal.

NOTE: In case a married couple find that their Nakshatras belong to the inimical category of animals they should try to investigate if the cause of their matrimonial problems is indirectly caused by physical dissatisfaction and sexual incompatibility.

F. RAJJU/SPIRITUAL

Literally the word RAJJU means 'rope'. The purpose of this agreement is to establish the invisible spiritual bond that binds them together like a rope tied round them. This agreement relates to spiritual compatibility, a subtle rapport of the Chakras, the inner energy centres of the couple.

There are five 'ropes' binding at different levels of the subtle body:

1. *SIROH RAJJU- at the level of Ajana Chakra, head region.*
2. *GREEVA RAJJU-at the level of Vishuddha Chakra, neck region.*
3. *KATI RAJJU- combining the levels of Anahata, Manipura, waist level.*
4. *OORU RAJJU- at the level of Swadhishthana, thigh level.*
5. *PAADA RAJJU- at the level of Muladhara, foot level.*

The 27 Nakshatras are then allotted to these five levels. Three Nakshatras are allotted to the first SIROH RAJJU at the Ajana level which has governance over the whole body. Six Nakshatras are allotted to each of the four remaining Rajju groups divided into two parts called ascending and descending order representing the left and right side of the body. The Tabulation is as follows:

NAKSHATRAS AND RAJJU GROUPS

SIROH RAJJU	5, 14, 23	
	Ascending Order	Descending Order
GREEVA RAJJU	4, 13, 22	6, 15, 24
KATI RAJJU	3, 12, 21	7, 16, 25
OORU RAJJU	2, 11, 20	8, 17, 26
PADA RAJJU	1, 10, 19	9, 18, 27

RULE: *They should belong to different Rajju and different Order for agreement. If same Rajju but different Order or different Rajju same Order it is average agreement. If same Rajju and same Order there is no agreement.*

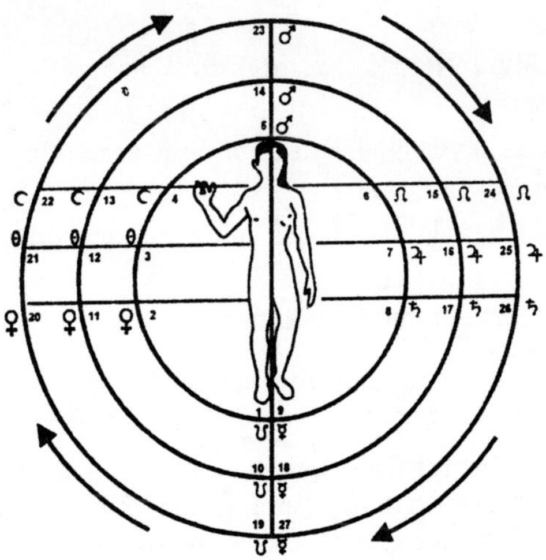

Critical Study: Let us have a critical look at this rule. If we observe the figure, in the centre we have the figure of the couple represented by half male and half female. There are three loops encircling this central figure. The vertical line passing through the head and through the feet cuts these three loops at six points, three above the head and three below the feet. Three lines parallel to each, one passing through the neck, one through the waist and the third through the thighs cut the loops each at six points, three on the right and three on the left.

Thus on each loop we have nine points of intersection. Starting with Nakshatra 1st at the right foot of the figure where the vertical line cuts the innermost loop we allot one Nakshatra at every intersection of the loop and line going in the clockwise direction. We continue to allot Nakshatras in the same way starting with Nakshatra 10th at the right foot on the intersection on the second loop and Nakshatra 19th on the third loop. I have also marked the planetary ruler of the Nakshatra by the side of the number. The arrows on the loops show the ascending and descending orders. We note that in this arrangement we get the same planetary rulers at the points of intersection on each line one each side. We also note:

1. At feet level Nakshatras of Ketu ascending, Mercury descending.
2. At thigh level Nakshatras of Venus ascending, Saturn descending.
3. At the waist level Nakshatras of Sun ascending, Jupiter descending.
4. At the neck level Nakshatras of Moon ascending, Rahu descending.
5. At the head level three Nakshatras of Mars.

We shall now try to understand the implication of the rule regarding RAJJU agreement.

The rule states that for Rajju agreement the Nakshatras of the couple should not belong to the same group. The next best is to belong to either different groups and same order or same group and different order.

From the figure it can be seen when the couple have Nakshatras that belong to the same group and same order they belong to

Nakshatras having the same Planetary ruler. The sages obviously felt that would cause problems for the couple. Planetary energies connected to the Subtle Chakra energies could not be alike. Probably 'like energies repel'. If the couple belong to the same group but different order the planetary rulers would be different for their Nakshatras. Similarly if they belong to different group but same order they would belong to Nakshatras with different planetary rulers. 'Unlike energies attract'

The planetary allotment also seems to have been on the basis of harmony between a planet's energy and the Chakra energy. The energy of Mars has some harmony with the energy aspect of Ajna Chakra. Moon and Rahu have energies that are in harmony with two different energies in Vishuddha Chakra. Similarly the energies of the other planets are in harmony with certain energy aspects of corresponding Chakras. Like the magnetic energy principle, 'like poles repel', if the same Chakra energy pattern is present in both as indicated by their Nakshatras having the same planetary rulers, there could be some kind of 'repulsion' on the Chakra energy. The person with the weaker Chakra would suffer or at least there would be some trouble between the couple arising out of this repulsion.

This RAJJU agreement appears to be based purely on consideration of compatibility of the 'Subtle Energy Fields' of the couple. It ensures that there is no 'mutual repulsion' at the inner Chakra energy level. It ensures inner agreement and spiritual harmony. Thus indirectly it ensures physical well-being, good health, mental peace and happiness in the marriage as the Chakra energies we have seen are connected with the mental and physical aspects as well.

The Subtle energy flowing on the left and right sides of the human body is not the same. In the next Nakshatra agreement rule this is fully explained. In the figure we note that the planets in the ascending order are on the right side and those in the descending order are on the left side. If the Nakshatras of the couple belong to different orders one will have 'right side energy' while the other will have 'left side energy'. This ensures compatibility based on the magnetic principle 'Unlike poles attract each other'. Thus the ideal combination would be both for the Chakra energy and the right or left side energy qualities to be unlike in the couple to create greater 'Subtle Chakra' Energy attraction, strength and bonding at a spiritual level. As the couple are in close rapport most of the time and particularly during sexual union if there is repulsion in their inner energies in due course problems will arise in one of them or both. When trouble starts for 'no apparent reason', the 'reason' may be in the incompatibility of the Inner Subtle Energies. I shall now discuss the consequences of incompatibility of each RAJJU.

1. Pada Rajju:

If both the partners belong to the same group of Nakshatras of this RAJJU there will be incompatibility at this level. The Chakra connected to this level is the Muladhara, related to element earth. It is the base Chakra. It is connected with stability and steadfastness. Therefore one of the partners could become psychologically 'unstable'. The person becomes restless and develops a desire to 'wander away', 'drift'. Consciously or unconsciously the person will create circumstances that keep them away from each other.

2. Ooru Rajju:

This RAJJU is related to the Swadhishthana Chakra, related to the element water. It is connected with fecundity and creativity of the individual. In case, the couple have their Nakshatras within the same group and same order there will be constant repulsion of the energies related to this Chakra and also the energies of the left or right side. This may in due course lead to sexual problems on the physical or psychological level . There may be a feeling of frustration. The subtle or sublime experience of sexual satisfaction will be denied. Gradually the interest will decline. On the mental level creative faculties may get gradually effected. Concentration may be lost. The interest in creative activities will diminish.

As a result of loss of concentration and application even professional activity may suffer. Eventually the material prosperity is also effected.

3. Kati Rajju:

The two Chakras Manipura related to element fire and Anahata related to air are connected to this RAJJU. The functions of the heart, the circulation, the stomach, the digestive and excretory systems are related to the energies of these Chakras. The entire region from the heart to the pelvic comes under the Subtle energy of these Chakras.

If the Nakshatras of the couple are for example in the sets 3, 12, 21 or 7, 16,25 they belong to the same group and same order. There will be repulsion of the Subtle energy leading to problems connected with this region. These problems may be connected with the functioning of the heart and circulation. There may be impairment of the digestive system. The excretory system may lose its efficiency. Appetite may be lost. On the mental level it may lead to states of anxiety, tension, feelings of insecurity, unreasonable fear and similar complexes. Loss of courage and confidence will lead to lack if initiative and hesitation in taking up responsibilities. Each one of the partners may develop some of these problems not necessarily the same or all of them.

4. Greeva Rajju:

This is connected to the energies of Vishuddha Chakra related to the element ether. Being at the throat region the Subtle Energy of this Chakra is responsible for the proper function of the respiratory system. The functions of speech, breathing, tasting and all parts of the mouth and throat region are under the domain of this Chakra.

If the Nakshatras of the couple for example belong to the set 4,13,22 or 6,15,24 then they both belong to the same group of this Rajju and also the same order. There is therefore a repulsion of the Subtle energies at this level. One of the partners may find the conversation of the other very uninteresting, rude and without affection. The intentions of one will not be clear to the other. There will be frequent misunderstanding.

This may lead to serious marital problems. There may be a general diminishing of the efficiency of sense-organs and decrease in the pleasure of eating. Most important is the possibility of problems of the respiratory system. Since this is related to the essential function for sustaining life, this RAJJU agreement seems to have a special importance. It is possibly because of this implication some of the classical texts on the subject mention that disagreement on this level can lead to curtailment of longevity.

Though it is not always the case, we should certainly realize that RAJJU agreements have to be carefully noted and given due importance.

5. Siroh Rajju:

The Chakra connected with this RAJJU is the Ajna , located between the eye brows. It is associated with the mind, the seat of emotions, motivations, memories, impulses, discrimination, desires and feelings. Negative emotions of anger and violence also come under this Chakra. Since several psychosomatic problems are related to the mind this Chakra energy is important for physical well-being in general.

When the couple have their Nakshatras in the same set 5,14,23 there is Rajju disagreement. The ruling planet of these Nakshatras is Mars, the planet of anger, quick temper and violence. The repulsion caused to the Subtle energies at this level may lead to fits of temper and unreasonable anger in one of the partners. Consequently there may be violent incidents. One of them may develop the desire to go astray, to cheat on the other, to be unfaithful.Prejudice and antagonism will develope between the couple. At times there may be a compulsive desire to be promiscuous or indulge in extra marital relationship. Not only does the person who develops these subconscious behavior patterns suffers, but also creates misery to the life partner. The relationship begins to get eroded.

Since RAJJU agreement is related to Planetary energies, the Subtle energies of the Chakras and the energies on the right and left side of the body some of the classical works mention that this agreement is one of the most important agreements.

G. NADI/SPIRITUAL

NADI literally means 'nerve' In Yoga, Nadi is used to mean the channels of energy. The paths along which energy of the Subtle Body travels are called Nadis. There are several Nadis among which three are considered important. They are *IDA, PINGALA AND SUSHUMNA.* All of these start at the base Muladhara Chakra. The Nadi Pingala starts on the right side and Ida on the left side of this Chakra. They terminate at the Ajna Chakra.

Sushumna Nadi travels straight, right through the centre of the Chakras thus forming a channel through the Chakras. The energy from below the Base Chakra rises up and travels through this Nadi. Ida and Pingala which are on the left and right sides of the body respectively form channels that appear to move in a serpentine path, moving from left to right and right to left forming circles around each Chakra.

In the figure on the next page I have shown Pingala as a straight channel on the right of the body and Ida a straight channel on the left side of the body, with Sushumna in the centre. Since the power at the base is described as a sleeping serpent and the rising of this energy as a serpent rising, I have drawn two serpents rising from the base. The strait lines representing the channels cut these serpents at several points. I have placed the numbers of the Nakshatras at these points starting from the left intersection at the bottom, going round each circle.

You will see that the Nakshatras related to each Nadi is as follows:

1. Ida: 1, 6, 7, 12, 13, 18 ,19, 24, 25.
2. Sushumna: 2, 5, 8, 11, 14, 17, 20, 23, 26.
3. Pingala : 3, 4, 9, 10, 15, 16, 21, 22, 27.

RULE: *The Nakshatras of the couple should not fall in the same Nadi group.*

I shall now discuss in detail the implications of this rule and how it actually effects the energies based on yogic concepts of the Nadis.

The figure shows not only the numbers at the points of intersection but also the planets ruling the Nakshatras. It is interesting to note that in the central channel we have the Nakshatras ruled by Saturn, Mars and Venus. We have seen this grouping of the Nakshatras in the Mahendra agreement. The energies on the right and left are considered to be masculine and feminine energies represented by Purusha and Prakriti or Shiva and his consort Parvati. In the central Channel, Nakshatras ruled by Mars represent masculine energy, those by Venus feminine energy and those by Saturn, neutral. Hence Sushumna actually represents the integration of the masculine and feminine energy.

To understand the logic or rationale behind the rule I have

NADI - NAKSHATRA MANDALA CHART

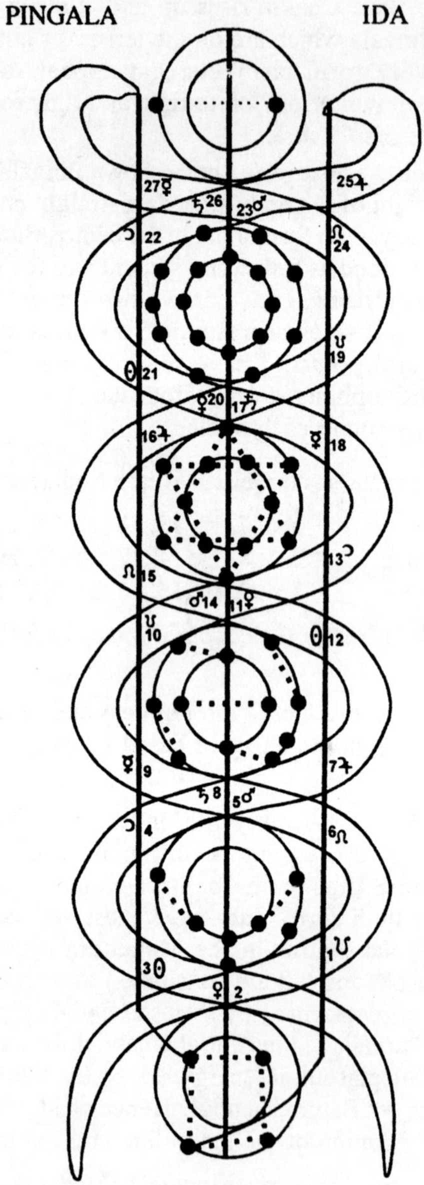

evolved an illustrative process. In this illustrative proof :

1. The male principle, Pingala Energy is represented by a vertical white triangle.
2. The female principle, Ida energy is represented by an inverted dark triangle.
3. When these two combine and a neutral energy is evolved I represent this by imposing the white triangle on the dark triangle. We then have a six vertex star, which represents balance and harmony.

While the energies in the Sushumna are the combined neutral energies in the human being as a whole all energies are not neutralized. There is a domination of masculine energy or feminine energy in both male and female. This male and female energy we speak of here should not be confused with normal male and female sexuality. To represent the human being I have adopted a set of three triangles. The human male is represented by two vertical white triangles with one black inverted triangle in the centre. Similarly to represent the human female I use threc triangles, two inverted dark triangles with one vertical white triangle at the centre. When the pure male principle and pure female principle join together, we have the three harmonious six vertex stars formed by the super imposition of the white over the black triangle.

However human beings are not just the pure principles.There are men dominated by either the energy of Ida or Pingala or Sushumna. Similarly there are females dominated by one of these energies. A male belonging to an ida is considered an Ida male. A man born in Pingala Nakshatra is considered a Pingala Male. In the same way we have the Ida and Pingala female and the Sushumna male and Sushumna female. I represent the Ida dominated man by the usual male symbol of three triangles, two vertical white with a black inverted triangle in the middle *plus* an extra inverted dark triangle. A pingala dominated male would have a white vertical triangle added and a Sushumna dominated male would have a six vertex black and white star added.

Similarly for the female dominated by Ida energy, I have used the usual female principle symbol of two inverted black triangles with a vertical white triangle in the centre *plus* a dark inverted triangle. For the Pingala dominated I add a white vertical and for the Sushumna dominated I add a six vertex black and white star.

Having established our symbols on the basis of the energy structure we shall study all the possible cases. They are :

1. An Ida Nakshatra male joins an Ida Nakshatra female.
2. An Ida Nakshatra male joins a Pingala Nakshatra female.
3. A Pingala Nakshatra male joins an Ida Nakshatra female.
4. A Pingala Nakshatra male joins a Pingala Nakshatra female.
5. A Sushumna Nakshatra male joins an Ida Nakshatra female.
6. A Sushumna Nakshatra male joins a Pingala Nakshatra female.
7. An Ida Nakshatra male joins a Sushumna Nakshatra female.
8. A Pingala Nakshatra male joins a Sushumna Nakshatra female.
9. A Sushumna Nakshatra male joins a Sushumna Nakshatra female.

I have illustrated these nine combinations with the symbols adopted and when the triangles are merged to form the harmonious six vertex black and white stars, we find that in some combinations either white vertical triangles are black inverted triangles remain unbalanced while some are balanced. Study the following figure :

BASIC SYMBOLS

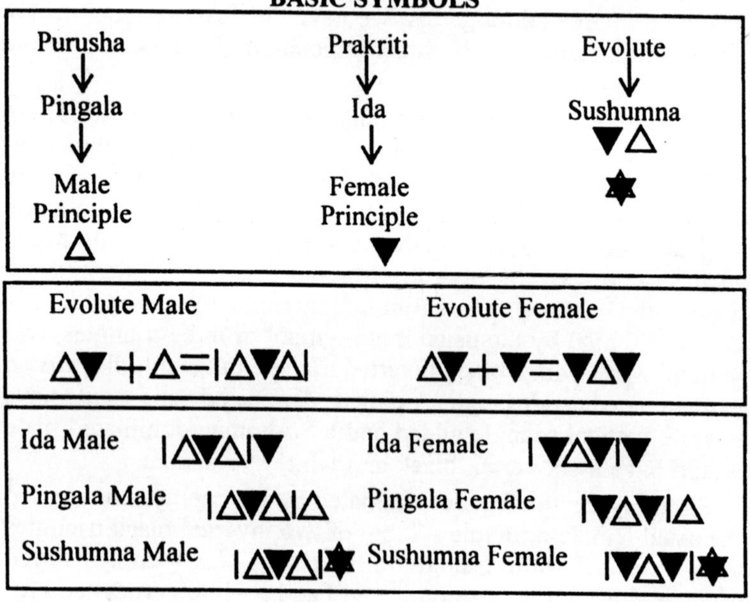

COMBINATIONS

<table>
<tr><td>1. Ida Male
|△▼△|▼</td><td>+</td><td>Ida Female
|▼△▼|▼</td><td>Male
✡✡</td><td>+</td><td>Female
✡▼▼</td><td>Unbalanced</td></tr>
<tr><td>2. Ida Male
|△▼△|▼</td><td>+</td><td>Pingala Female
|▼△▼|△</td><td>Male
✡✡</td><td>+</td><td>Female
✡✡</td><td>Balanced</td></tr>
<tr><td>3. Pingala Male
|△▼△|△</td><td>+</td><td>Ida Female
|▼△▼|▼</td><td>Male
△△✡</td><td>+</td><td>Female
▼▼✡</td><td>✡✡✡✡
Balanced</td></tr>
<tr><td>4. Pingala Male
|△▼△|△</td><td>+</td><td>Pingala Female
|▼△▼|△</td><td>Male
△△✡</td><td>+</td><td>Female
✡✡</td><td>Unbalanced</td></tr>
<tr><td>5. Sushumna Male
|△▼△|✡</td><td>+</td><td>Ida Female
|▼△▼|▼</td><td>Male
✡✡△</td><td>+</td><td>Female
✡▼▼</td><td>Unbalanced</td></tr>
<tr><td>6. Sushumna Male
|△▼△|✡</td><td>+</td><td>Pingala Female
|▼△▼|△</td><td>Male
✡✡△</td><td>+</td><td>Female
✡✡</td><td>Unbalanced</td></tr>
<tr><td>7. Ida Male
|△▼△|▼</td><td>+</td><td>Sushumna Female
|▼△▼|✡</td><td>Male
✡✡</td><td>+</td><td>Female
✡✡▼</td><td>Unbalanced</td></tr>
<tr><td>8. Pingala Male
|△▼△|△</td><td>+</td><td>Sushumna Female
|▼△▼|✡</td><td>Male
✡△△</td><td>+</td><td>Female
✡✡▼</td><td>Unbalanced</td></tr>
<tr><td>9. Sushumna Male
|△▼△|✡</td><td>+</td><td>Sushumna Female
|▼△▼|✡</td><td>Male
✡✡△</td><td>+</td><td>Female
✡✡▼</td><td>✡✡✡✡✡
Balanced</td></tr>
</table>

Where I Beg to Differ

Before I go to the study of the results of the various combinations I should state that some Vedic astrological scholars for very good reason have taken the meaning of Nadi as 'blood vessel'. In Ayurveda, the Indian science of health and longevity, there are methods of determining the perturbation in the three subtle functional humours of the body Vata, Pitta and Kapha by examining the pulse (Nadi).

If this meaning is attributed to the Nadi and each group of Nakshatras identified with one of the Doshas (Humours), Vata, Pitta and Kapha the significance of the rule is apparent. It is not advisable that both partners should belong to the same predominant constitution Vata, Pitta or Kapha. It is better the couple belong to two different constitutions for their own health and the health of their offspring.

I beg to differ in this approach to the Nadi rule. Generally in the classics the Nadis are referred as *Parsva Nadi* (Side Nadi) and *Madhyama Nadi* (Central Nadi). This is more relevant to the Nadi in Yoga than the simple meaning of blood vessels and establishing a connection to the physical state. The spiritual aspect of the human being was never overlooked by sages and certainly rules that decide the suitability of a union cannot overlook the spiritual aspect. The two rules Rajju and Nadi in my considered opinion belong to the spiritual areas of comparison. Only then these two rules assume greater significance. For example, an obese person is generally considered a Kapa dominant personality. I cannot see any major catastrophe befalling an obese woman marrying an obese man!

With due apologies to the learned scholars of Vedic astrology who follow this interpretation I proceed to study the results of the different Nadi combinations and come to the conclusion, which I think should be the proper interpretation of the rule given by the sages. The sages rarely clarified the exceptions and inclusions to the general rule and left it to the understanding of the versatile astrologer.

Results of different Combinations :

Case 1. Ida Male + Ida Female: We can see from the illustration that the Male gets balanced. Hence this combination results in some energy disturbance of the female.

Case 2. Ida Male + Pingala Female: The illustration shows that both the Male and Female are individually balanced and therefore the union will also be balanced.

Case 3. Pingala Male + Ida Female: Here we find that though the individual Male and Female are not balanced on account of the increase in the elements, the combination however brings a balance, which only means that the elements that bring over the mutual attraction and dependence, increase in this relationship bringing fulfilment through the union.

Case 4. Pingala Male + Pingala Female: We note that the Male is unbalanced, while the Female is balanced. Hence the union will be unbalanced with the male having some energy disturbance.

Case 5. Sushumna Male + Ida Female: In this combination both the Male and female are unbalanced, and the union cannot be balanced.

Case 6. Sushumna Male + Pingala Female: Here the Male is unbalanced but the female is balanced. Naturally the union cannot be balanced.

Case 7. Ida Male + Sushumna Female: In this combination the Male is balanced and the female unbalanced, and the union cannot be balanced.

Case 8. Pingala Male + Sushumna Female: Here also both the Male and the female are unbalanced. The union is not balanced.

Case 9. Sushumna Male + Sushumna Female: In this case the transfer of elements to the male and female equalizes their position and the union is eventually balanced.

Hence in the 9 possibilities case 2, case 3 and case 9, are the only balanced combinations. Hence the original rule could be best stated as:

Both partners should belong to the same Sushumna or they should belong to different Nadis of Ida and Pingala to have Nadi agreement.

In all the remaining cases either one of them or both will have problems of health, a feeling that the partner is aggressive and demanding or in certain extreme cases the partner becoming disloyal and promiscuous.

H. GANA/SPIRITUAL

In this asterism comparison, the Nakshatras are divided again into three groups. The groups are called DEVA, MANUSHYA and RAKSHASA. DEVA means Gods. MANUSHYA means Humans. RAKSHASAS means Demons. The Nakshatras allotted to the three categories are as follows:

DEVA • Nos. 1,5,7,8,13,15,17,22,27.
MANUSHYA • Nos. 2,4,6,11,12,20,21,25,26.
RAKSHASA • Nos. 3,9,10,14,16,18,19,23,24.

RULE: *The couple should have Nakshatras that fall in the same category, that is both should be Deva or both should be Manushya or both should be Rakshasa. Such a combination is considered the best.*

If one is Deva and the other Manushya the combination is *good.*
If one is Manushya and the other Rakshasa it is *bad.*
If one is Deva and the other is Rakshasa it is *worst.*

Critical Study: The names given to the three categories need not make one feel that one set of nine Nakshatras have been unduly elevated to the position of Gods and another set condemned to the position of Demons. It is not that those with the Moon in the Nakshatras under category one are gods. They are very much human beings as the rest of their fellow beings. However, this naming is done to enable us to understand certain categorization easily.

Thus the word Devas has to be associated with qualities such as patience, mercy, understanding, broad-mindedness, forgiving, cooperating. The word Manushyas has to be associated with pleasure, comfort, materialism, possessiveness, desire, security, while the word Rakshasas has to be associated with aggressiveness, haste, domination, lust, vengeance and similar qualities. The categorization is made on the basis of these and other similar qualities.

In Hindu Philosophy there are three GUNAS (Qualities) namely *Sattva, Rajas and Tamas.* A simplistic way of explaining is to say that these are the basic qualitative energies from which the universe evolved. The qualities attributed to the *Devas* (Gods) may be identified with Sattva; those of *Manushya* (Humans) with Rajas and those of *Rakshasas* (Demons) with Tamas. Since the terms Sattva, Rajas, and Tamas are terms used in Hindu Philosophy and not generally known or understood by the common man, the sages preferred to use the common terms Deva, Manushya, and Rakshasa, meaning *Gods*, Humans and Demons, terms which everyone can understand. In every human being there is the God, the Human and the Demon. However, these three qualities are not necessarily balanced. One quality may dominate and take precedence over the others. That is to say there is Sattva, Rajas and Tamas Gunas in everyone but one of the Guna may dominate the person. If Sattva dominates we call the person a Sattvic person. One who has dominance of Rajas is called a Rajasic person and one who has an excess of Tamas, a Tamasic person.

A division has to be made of the 27 Nakshatras into the three categories indicating that those born under a particular Nakshatra are likely to have a particular Guna prominent. Among the planets, Guru and Chandra are associated with *Sattva*; Shukra and Budha with *Rajas*, Rahu, Ketu, Kuja and Shani with *Tamas*. There is a slight difference in the allocation of Surya, some attributing Sattva, some Rajas. My opinion is that Surya in fact has all the three Gunas but is dominated by Rajas, and for the purpose of categorization it is best to put it under Rajas.

Thus we see that we have only two planets Guru and Chandra for Sattva, three planets Surya, Shukra and Budha for Rajas and four planets Shani, Kuja, Rahu and Ketu for Tamas.

I presume that based on the sign in which the Nakshatra falls, the relationship between the Nakshatra Lord and the Sign Lord, the Lords of the Padas of the Nakshatras and their relationship with the Sign Lord, the sages in their wisdom, allotted the Nakshatras to the three categories as given.

Here it should be noted that a Nakshatra whose Lord is a Tamas planet having been judged by the Sages to have more of Sattva qualities on account of other factors, has been allotted to the Deva category.

It is always better to unite those with the same GUNA, that is the same qualities. This will enable them to have a common attitude and approach to daily problems and the routine of life. For in Vedic comparison astrology it is stated that if there is no agreement under this head there will be daily quarrels between the couple. This is because of the difference of approach to common situations in the life of the couple. Disagreement in this category provokes conflict.

For example, if a neighbor behaved with some indiscretion, the Sattvic partner would want to forgive and forget while the Tamasic partner would want to retaliate. This would cause friction. But if both were Sattvic or both Tamasic there would be no conflict in their reaction to what the neighbor did. They would move in unison. This would not only avoid friction between them but also enhance their mutual understanding.

If the ideal of both belonging to the same category is not possible the next best is Deva and Manushya combination. This is because the Manushya partner may very well respond to the attitude of the Sattvic partner. When Deva and Rakshasa are united it is two persons with extreme attitudes trying to work together. It would be constant combat. However, occasionally they may strike a compromise in their approach. But when Manushya and Rakshasa combine, the Rakshasa partner will always have the final word and the Manushya partner will miserably fail in getting his or her point of view appreciated and this can certainly lead to a lot of problems.

CHAPTER 9

Petal 4

Comparison of Karmic Content The Challenges of Life

We have seen that for Astrological delineation purposes the planets Sun, Mars, Saturn, Rahu and Ketu are considered 'Natural Malefic'. The remaining four Venus, Jupiter, Mercury and Moon are considered 'Natural Benefic' though some conditions are attached to Mercury and Moon to become benefic.

It is the malefic planets that determine the Karmic Negative Destiny of a person. The trials and tribulations of life, the difficulties and obstructions and the challenges one meets are all the results of Karma. These are all seen in a chart from the position and condition of the malefic planets.

RULE:

The synastry rule is that the Malefic Content in the charts of the couple should be equal. In any case the malefic content in one should not be less than 75% of the malefic content of the other. Between 50% and 75% it is considered average but below 50% it is considered incompatible.

This Percentage can be calculated from the formula:

$$\frac{\textit{Malefic Content in the Female chart}}{\textit{Malefic Content in the Male chart}} \times 100$$

This rule leads us to two questions:

1. How to measure the Karmic content in a chart?
2. Why equality of the Karmic content is considered ideal?

Let us consider the first question. If we establish some kind of units to measure the Karmic contents and measure the contents in the two charts with the same measuring units we will be able to arrive at comparative figures. The sages have given us such a system.

I give below a chart of units, by the help of which we can arrive at comparative figures:

MALEFIC CONTENT UNITS

*Sign No	Planet	Very friendly	Friendly	Own neutral	Moola trikona	Exal-tation	Enemy	Very inimical	Debili-tated
2 or 4 or 12	☉	3	4	8	9	12	14	15	16
	☊ ♄ ☋	6	8	16	18	24	28	30	32
	♂	9	12	24	27	36	42	45	48
1 or 7 or 8	☉	12	16	32	36	48	56	60	64
	☊ ♄ ☋	24	32	64	72	96	112	120	128
	♂	36	48	96	108	144	168	180	192

* *Sign counted from Lagna or Chandra or Shukra*

Let us first understand the system of allotment of units. The principle of allotment of values is as follows:

1. The malefic planets are graded. Sun is considered the least malefic, Saturn, Rahu, Ketu are more malefic and Mars is the most malefic. This gradation is for Synastry purposes only as affecting matrimonial affairs.

2. Hence in giving malefic value units, Saturn, Rahu, Ketu are given double the value of Sun and Mars is given treble the value of Sun.

3. These malefic planets are considered more malefic when in the 1st, 7th, or 8th signs from the Ascendent sign or Moon Sign or Venus Sign than when they are in 2nd, 4th, or 12th signs from these signs.

4. The malefic value in these signs varies according to the net relationship of the planet to the sign. This relationship is in 8 grades. The least malefic sign is the sign which is very friendly. The malefic value steadily increases as the sign is Friendly to

the planet, Own/Neutral, Moola Trikona, Exaltation, Enemy, Very Inimical and finally Debilitated. Starting with the first the gradation is in the ratio 1, $1\frac{1}{3}$, $2\frac{2}{3}$, 3, 4, $4\frac{2}{3}$, 5, $5\frac{1}{3}$.

5. For convenience we shall take the minimum malefic value in a chart given by Sun if it is in the 2nd or 4th or 12th sign to be 3 units, to eliminate the fractions if that sign is a friendly sign to Sun. Then as per the ratio its malefic content units in the remaining type of signs will be 4, 8, 9, 12, 14, 15 and 16.
6. The values under each column for Rahu, Ketu and Saturn are double the values of Sun and for Mars the values are treble.
7. In the second half of the table where the planets are either in the 1st, 7th or 8th signs, which are considered more malefic places the values for Sun are 4 times those of Sun in the top half.
8. In the second half the values for Rahu, Ketu and Saturn are double the values for Sun and for Mars the values are treble.

We have now constructed a table of values satisfying the basic principles given in rules 1 to 3.

It should be noted that the ratios, the increases in the malefic content for certain planets and for certain signs given in this table is just conveniently fixed to meet the requirements of the principles. Any suitable starting value, any increasing gradation may be used and another table prepared on the basis of which the malefic contents of the two charts may be established and compared. The percentage and ratio are bound to be the same.

Here it must be noted that the table enables us to find the malefic content in the two charts based on the same scale of evaluation and helps us compare their malefic contents.

NOTE: *Students of Vedic Astrology should note that this method of evaluating the Karmic malefic content of Sun, Rahu, Ketu, Saturn and Mars, should be used only for purposes of synastry. The technique should not be used for any general assessment of the Karmic level in a horoscope chart. It would be an irresponsible generalization of a principle that has a specific application.*

Let us get to an example.

The charts of the couple are:

FEMALE BORN ON

21-12-1954 AT 8h-25m G.M.T., AT 12°-58' N.Lat. 77°-36' E. Long.

<table>
<tr><td></td><td>Asnd 4</td><td></td><td>Ketu 12</td></tr>
<tr><td>Mars 19</td><td rowspan="2" colspan="2">Rashi Chart</td><td>Jupiter (R) 9</td></tr>
<tr><td></td><td></td></tr>
<tr><td>Sun 5
Mercury 1
Rahu 12</td><td></td><td>Moon 22
Saturn 23
Venus 25</td><td></td></tr>
</table>

MALE BORN ON 21-01-1955 at 01h-02m G.M.T at 13°-04' N.Lat and 80°-15' E. Long.

<table>
<tr><td>Mars 11</td><td></td><td></td><td>Ketu 12</td></tr>
<tr><td></td><td rowspan="2" colspan="2">Rashi Chart</td><td>Jupiter(R) 9</td></tr>
<tr><td>Asnd 5
Sun 5
Mercury 23</td><td></td></tr>
<tr><td>Moon 2
Rahu 12</td><td>Venus 20</td><td>Saturn 26</td><td></td></tr>
</table>

Stage 1.

First prepare tables showing the number of the sign position from Lagna, Moon and Venus for the five malefic planets in both the Charts.

MALE CHART

	FROM LAGNA	FROM MOON	FROM VENUS
SURYA	***1ST POSITION**	***2nd POSITION**	3rd POSITION
SHANI	10th POSITION	11th POSITION	***12th POSITION**
RAHU	***12th POSITION**	***1st POSITION**	***2nd POSITION**
KETU	6th POSITION	***7th POSITION**	***8th POSITION**
KUJA	3rd POSITION	***4th POSITION**	5th POSITION

FEMALE CHART

	FROM LAGNA	FROM CHANDRA	FROM SHUKRA
SURYA	9TH POSITION	3rd POSITION	3rd POSITION
SHANI	***7th POSITION**	***1st POSITION**	***1st POSITION**
RAHU	9th POSITION	3rd POSITION	3rd POSITION
KETU	3rd POSITION	9th POSITION	9th POSITION
KUJA	11th POSITION	5th POSITION	5th POSITION

*In the above we only take the positions relevant for evaluating the malefic content. These are 1,2,4,7,8 and 12 marked by **

Stage 2.

Then prepare the sign position for the five planets for both Male and Female charts.

<u>Male Chart:</u> Sun is in Capricorn ruled by Saturn, natural enemy... E
Saturn is in Libra, Exalted

Rahu is in Sagit. ruled by Jupiter, natural enemy ... E

Ketu is in Gemini ruled by Mercury, natural enemy ... E
Mars is in Pisces ruled by Jupiter,., natural friend F

Stage 3.

Prepare the net relationship for the five planets in their respective positions.

Saturn is in 10th from Sun and hence is a temporary friend for Sun.

Net position of Sun is E + T. F = Neutral .. N

Net position of Saturn... Exalted. (sign relationship not relevant)

Jupiter is in the 8th from Rahu and hence temporary enemy for Rahu.

Net position of Rahu is N + T. E = Enemy.... E.

Mercury is in the 8th from Ketu and hence temporary enemy.

Net position of Ketu is E + T. E = Very Inimical... V..E.

Jupiter is in the 5th from Mars hence temporary enemy.

Net position of Mars is F + T. E = Neutral............. .N.

Stage 4.

Taking the corresponding unit values for these planets from the MALEFIC CONTENT UNITS TABLE on page 98. Insert these values based on the relevant positions indicated in table of Stage 1.

For example, in the Male Chart Surya is in 1st position from Lagna. In the Units Table see in the lower half which gives values for positions 1 or 7 or 8. See in the row opposite Surya and under Neutral which is the net position of Surya. The value is 32. From Moon it is in 2nd position .Now see from the upper half of the Table which gives values for positions 2 or 4 or 12 under Neutral. The value is 8. Then come to Shani. The only relevant position is 12th from Venus. See in the upper half in the row for Shani and in the column under Exalted. The value is 24. Rahu is 12th from Lagna, 1st from Moon, 2nd from Venus which are the relevant positions. The value for 12 and 2nd positions under enemy is 28. For Rahu in the 1st position see lower half of table under column Enemy. The value is 112. Ketu is 7th from Moon and 8th from Venus. In the lower half in the row of Ketu under column Very Inimical the value is 120. Mars is in 4th position from Moon, the only relevant position. In the upper half in row of Mars under the column Neutral we have value 24. All these values are tabulated.

MALE CHART MALEFIC CONTENT UNITS

	From Asnd	From Moon	From Venus
Sun	32	8	
Saturn			24
Rahu	28	112	28
Ketu		120	120
Mars		24	
TOTAL	60 +	264 +	172

= 496

Similarly Female Chart Malefic Content Units could be prepared in four stages. However as your experience increases it will be possible to work out all the stages in one table as follows:

FEMALE CHART MALEFIC CONTENT UNITS

	From Asnd	From Moon	From Venus
Sun			
Saturn	Exalt = 96	Exalt = 96	Exalt = 96
Rahu			
Ketu			
Mars			
TOTAL	96 +	96 +	96

= 288

Except Saturn no other planet is in any relevent afflicting position.

We do not consider Saturn is in Libra ruled by Venus which is a Friend. Venus is placed in the same sign as Saturn hence it becomes a Temporary Enemy. We only consider Saturn is in Exalt.

Comparison of Malefic Contents:

$$\frac{\textit{Female Malefic Content Units}}{\textit{Male Malefic Content Units}} \times 100$$

$$\frac{288}{496} \times 100 = 50.8\%$$

Why is equality of Karmic content considered ideal?

The Karmic content in a chart calculated as above is a measure of the Negative Karma or Challenges the individual would face in connection with married life, companionship and harmony in the same. Obviously the individual in whose chart the malefic content is high will face many challenges. If this individual is linked to a partner whose chart shows a very low Challenge level how would it be possible for them to travel together as life companions? It would be like fixing two unequal wheels to a cart.

It would be a frustrating and frictional combination. As a couple living together they share life, its fortunes and failures equally. How can they realize their respective conjugal karmas together if the levels are so wide apart? Hence equality or near equality in the Karmic content is aimed at. The principle probably is that the couple deeply in love, attached to each other and determined to share and share alike, voyaging through life would be able to 'sink or sail' together.

CHAPTER 10

Petal 5

Planetary Cycles

COMPARISON BY PLANETARY PERIODS

Apart from basic characteristics in the chart of the partners that influence the course of material life, the cycles through which the couple pass through during the early years of marital life are important.

For this purpose the planetary cycle at the time of birth of both the partners has to be calculated. Add the subsequent cycles till you arrive at the period in which they would be getting married and the periods immediately thereafter.

RULE: *It is preferable that changes of major planetary cycles for the couple do not take place simultaneously, that is within an year. Also the lords of the Dasha through which the couple pass should not be mutually in positions that are either 6/8 or 2/12 to each other.*

The above two rules ensure that the planetary cycles through which the couple pass during and immediately after marriage do not create any sudden imbalances in their fortunes.

At the commencement of any major Dasha an individual undergoes major changes. Sometimes there are very important and radical changes in many aspects of life. These changes are not only in the material affairs but are also in the mental and psychological levels. At the commencement of a new Dasha individuals may change their attitude, behavior and outlook. Preferences and priorities may change. If at the same time the life partner is also entering a major Dasha and experiences similar changes there can be an upheaval in the family, its circumstances and in the psychological relationship of the partners. To avoid this it is advised to match charts where such coincidence of Dasha change does not take place.

When both partners are born in the same Nakshatras and padas this will naturally happen. This has to be avoided. So also every 10th and 19th Nakshatra counted from any Nakshatra has the same Dashas.

The second part of the rule ensures that the couple run planetary cycles, where the planets are not placed in mutually hostile positions to each other in their charts.

The importance of this Dasha comparison is apparent but cannot supersede the basic comparisons, given in Petals 1 to 5. When you have a long journey to make, you not only check up and ensure that your automobile is in good condition but also the road along which you travel is safe and sound. Similarly it is not only necessary that the charts of the couple basically agree, but also necessary that the future Planetary Cycles through which they pass through should be harmonious.

EXAMPLE:

Let us presume that the date of birth of the Male is 23rd February 1948 at 5.30 Am. Indian standard Time at Latitude 22°-35' North and Longitude 88°-23' East, (G.M.T = 0 Hours.)

From the Ephemeris it can be seen that the Moon is 15°-38' in Kataka (Cancer). This indicates that at the time of birth he had a balance of 1 year, 5 months, and 20 days of the Dasha of Saturn.

Let us presume that the Female was born on the 3rd June 1950 at 11.03 Am. Indian standard Time (G.M.T.= 05 Hrs 33 mts.) at Latitude 22°-35' North and longitude 88°-23' East. The Moon at the time of birth is 25°-20' in Dhanus. Hence the balance of Dasha at birth will be 6 months of Shukra.

MALE		FEMALE	
Date of Birth	1948 - 02 - 23	Date of Birth	1950 - 06 - 03
Balance of Saturn	1 - 05 - 20	Balance of Shukra	06 - -
	1949 - 08 - 13		1950 - 12 - 03
Dasha of Budha	17 - 00 - 00	Dasha of Surya	6 - 00 - 00
	1966 - 08 - 13		1956 - 12 - 03
Dasha of Kethu	7 - 00 - 00	Dasha Chandra	10 - 00 - 00
	1973 - 8 - 13		1966 - 12 - 03
Dasha of Shukra	20 - 00 - 00	Dasha of Kuja	7 - 00 - 00
	1993 - 8 - 13		1973 - 12 - 03
Dasha of Surya	6 - 00 - 00	Dasha of Rahu	18 - 00 - 00
	1999 - 8 - 13		1991 - 12 - 03
Dasha of Chandra	10 - 00 - 00	Dasha of Guru	16 - 00 - 00
	2009 - 8 - 13		2007 - 12 - 03

If the couple decided to get married around the year 1973 it can be seen that the male enters the Dasha of Venus on 13.8.1973 and the Female enters Rahu in the same year around December. After marriage both of them face a change of Dasha almost simultaneously.

Exception:

According to the rule connected with Dashas this is not advisable. However, if the Venus in the male chart is placed in a sign which is not malefic that is which is not the 6th, 8th, or 12th sign from the sign in which Rahu is found in the female chart, then the simultaneous change of Dasha may be over looked.

In this particular case the Venus of the Male is in the sign Pisces and Rahu of the female is also placed in Pisces hence the problems consequent to this coincidence of the Dasha change may be mitigated to some extent. This is more so because Venus is exalted in Pisces and Rahu is in neutral sign.

CHAPTER 11

Petal 6

Planetary Mutual Position

COMPARISON BY MUTUAL POSITIONS

The significant planets for comparison in Vedic astrology are:

Surya : The planet connected with the soul, good luck, fortune, vitality, health.

Chandra : Connected with the mind, psychology, motivations, health, longevity and fecundity.

Shukra : Significant of life partner, marriage, love, romance, sentiments.

Kuja : Emotional affairs, sexual urges, desires, matrimonial relationship.

Guru : Domestic and matrimonial happiness, children, prosperity and success in general.

In Vedic Astrology the 6th, 8th and 12th houses are considered malefic houses. These are normally counted from the Lagna sign and any planet placed in these houses its positive energy. Applying this rule to planetary relationships, the mutual 6th / 8th and 2nd/ 12th position between planets is considered unfavorable.

For example, in the chart of a Male if Guru is in the sign Tula and in the chart of a Female Kuja is in the sign Vrishabha, then it can be seen that Kuja is eighth from Guru and Guru is sixth from Kuja.

In assesing relationships a study of the mutual position of these five planets is made between the charts of the partners, that is the position of Surya in the male chart and the position of Surya in the female chart and similarly for the other four planets. If they are situated in malefic positions to each other then that planetary relationship is not favorable. For example, if Surya is in Simha for the male chart and Surya is in Kanya in the female chart, it is seen that the Male Surya is in 12th from the female Surya. Hence there is unfavorable relationship between the Suryas. Similarly it is seen for Chandra, Kuja, Shukra, and Guru.

For compatibility these planets should not be placed in mutually malefic positions. If all five are placed in malefic positions to each other there is no planetary agreement between charts. Possibly a disagreement up to two planets out of the five may be overlooked (40%). More than two planets in mutually malefic positions indicates possible disagreements and some material problems.

Let us take the charts of the male and the female given in petal 4.

FEMALE BORN 21.12.1954 at 8hr.25m GMT
Lat 12°-58' N, Long 77°-36' E

	Asnd		Ketu
Mars			Jup
Sun Mer Rahu			

MALE BORN 21.1.1955 at 1h-02m GMT
Lat 13°-04' N, Long 80°-15' E

Mars			Ketu
			Jup
Asnd. Sun Merc			
Rahu Moon	Ven	Sat	

We note that the male Sun is in the sign Capricorn and female Sun is in Sagittarius. Therefore, the male Sun is in the second to the female Sun sign and therefore, the female Sun Sign is in the 12th from the male Sun sign.

The Male Moon sign is in Sagittarius while the Female Moon is in Libra. Hence the Male Moon is third from the Female Moon and the Female Moon is the 11th from the Male Moon. It can be seen that Jupiter for both is in Cancer. Similarly the positions of Venus and Mars are found to be mutually 2/12. The results may be tabulated as follows:

SUN	MOON	MARS	VENUS	JUPITER
M2/F12	M3/F11	M2/F12	M2/F12	M1/F1

From the above table we note Planets Sun, Mars, Venus are mutually adverse.

I now give the possible results of the adverse placements to enable you to check up if the adverse results are counter balanced by any other favorable comparison rule so that agreement is assured.

SURYA: When Surya of the male happens to be in the 12th sign from the Surya sign of the Female, the male will cause some loss of confidence in the female, wound her ego, and on the physical level be a cause for devitalizing.

The same results are for the Male if the Surya of the female falls in the 12th of his own Surya sign.

If the Suryas of the male and female happen to be in signs that are mutually six and eight to each other there will be conflicts of egos, there may be health problems and lack of confidence.

CHANDRA: If the Male Moon sign happens to be the 12th from the Female Moon sign there will be psychological problems created by the male, who will also cause a lot of confusion, diffidence and uncertainty in her life. Unnecessary fears and suspicions may be created by him in her mind (For exception see under Rashi agreement).

The same results can be given for the male if the female Chandra Rashi is 12th from the Male Chandra Rashi.

If the Chandra Rasis are mutually six and eight to each other there will be problems of psychological disagreement between the couple. There will also be some affliction to the material well-being and also problems connected with or through progeny.

GURU: If the male Guru Sign is 12th from the female Guru Sign there will be some financial or material loss to the female from the male. There will also be some disharmony on the spiritual level. The male may be responsible for some problems through children for the female. The same results are given for the Male if the female Guru is in the 12th sign from Male Guru Sign. If the Guru Signs of the couple are mutually 6th and 8th the material level of the couple may be adversely effected.

There will be generally unhappiness and inner conflicts.The couple may have problems connected with birth or well-being of children.

SHUKRA : If the Male Shukra is 12th from the Female Shukra sign there will be emotional problems created for the female by the male. He will be the cause for some disappointments and she may feel want of deep feelings of attachment in their relationship.

The same happens to the Male if the Female Shukra sign is in the 12th from the Shukra sign of the male.

If the Shukra Signs are mutually 6th and 8th the relationship is not likely to be emotionally happy or contended. There may be a tendency to be mutually unfaithful to one another.

KUJA: If the Kuja sign of the male is the 12th from the female Kuja sign, the health and well-being of the female may be affected. There will be frequent quarrels and disputes with one or both partners being short tempered.

The same results come to the Male if the Female Kuja sign is in the 12th from the Male Kuja sign.

If the Kuja signs of the couple are mutually 6th and 8th, peace of the home will be lost due to constant quarrels, ill health, lack of physical compatibility and mutual aggressiveness. Physical violence is also a possibility.

SPECIAL NOTE: Some redeeming features are as follows:

SHUKRA-KUJA: With regard to the positions of Shukra and Kuja, in case they are adversely placed as indicated above you may look for a redeeming feature. That is check if the Shukra of one and the Kuja of the other are mutually in the 5th and 9th sign positions to each other. In this set up there will be good emotional and physical rapport between the couple, sufficient to off set any of the malefic indications given for Shukra and Kuja individually in each chart.

SUN- MOON- JUPITER: If any one of these is exalted in any one chart, the adverse indications given for it may be overlooked.(If any, one is debilitated the affliction is enhanced.)

CHAPTER 12

A Bird's Eye View

I now briefly summarize all the rules for ready reference:

Petal 1. Comparison of Position of Mars: Count the number of the sign in which Mars is placed both in the Female chart and Male chart. Count from the Ascendent, Moon and Venus to Mars both signs included. Tabulate as follows:

	From Asnd	From Moon	From Venus
Female Chart			
Male Chart			

Note also the Sign in which Mars is only in case it is in Gemini or Virgo. An evaluation procedure for deciding the level of Mars affliction (Kuja or Mangal Dosha) in a chart is as follows:

1. If in the 2nd or 4th from Ascendant affliction is: 20%
2. If in the 2nd or 4th from Ascendant and Moon or Venus: 30%
3. If in the 2nd or 4th from Ascendant and Moon and Venus: 40%
4. If in the 1st, 7th, 8th or 12th from the Ascendent: 50%
5. If it is either in 1st, 7th, 8th or 12th from Ascendent, and from Moon or Venus it affliction is: 60%
6. If it is either in 1st, 7th, 8th or12th from Ascendent and from Moon and also from Venus the affliction is: 70%
7. If it is in 1st, 7th, 8th or 12th from Ascendant which happens to be sign Gemini or Virgo affliction is: 80%
8. If it is in 1st, 7th, 8th or 12th from Ascendant and Moon or Venus which happens to be Gemini or Virgo affliction is: 90%
9. If it is in 1st, 7th, 8th, or 12th from Ascendant and Moon and Venus which happens to be Gemini or Virgo sign affliction is: 100%

RULE: *The percentage of affliction between the charts should be equal or not vary more than 10% to have agreement.*

Petal 2. Comparison of the position of Moon Signs:

RULE (a) : From female Moon Sign, male Moon sign in the 7th is best, 8th to 12 next best, 2nd to 6th is not good.

RULE (b) : The Lords of the Moon sign should be natural friends or neutral for agreement.

RULE (c) : Vashya agreement exists if for

Female Moon Sign	*Male Moon Sign*
Aries	Leo, Scorpio
Taurus	Cancer, Libra
Gemini	Virgo
Cancer	Scorpio, Sagitarius
Leo	Libra
Virgo	Pisces, Gemini
Libra	Capricorn
Scorpio	Cancer
Sagittarius	Pisces
Capricorn	Aries, Aquarius
Aquarius	Virgo
Pisces	Aries

Petal 3. Comparison on the basis of Nakshatras :

(a) Vedha : Nakshatras 1,2,3,4,5,6,7,8,9,10,11,12,13, are respectively opposed to 18,17,16,15, 14 and 23,22,21,20,19,27,26,25,24.

(b) Dina : Count from Female Nakshatra to Male Nakshatra both inclusive. Divide this number by 9. If the remainder is 1, 3, 5, or 7 there is no agreement. If it is 0,2,4,6, or 8 there is agreement.

(c) Stree Deerga : If count from Female Nakshatra to male Nakshatra is more than 15 it is the best agreement, between 8 and 14 it is good, 1 to 7 it is not good.

(d) Mahendra : If Male Nakshatra is 4th, 7th, 10th, 13th, 16th, 19th, 22nd or 25th from Female Nakshatra, there is agreement.

(e) Yoni	: The ideal combinations are
RULE	: *(1,24); (2,27); (3,8); (4,5); (6,19); (7,9) (10,11)*
	(12,26); (13,15); (14,16); (17,18); (20,22); (23,25); (21,21)

Note: In the above the first seven totally disagree respectively with the following seven combinations.

(f) Rajju	:	1st group. 5,14, 23		
			Ascending	Descending
		2nd group.	4,13,22	6,15,24.
		3rd group.	3,12,21	7,16,25.
		4th group.	2,11,20	8,17,26.
		5th group.	1,10,19	9,18,27.

RULE	: *Both should not belong to the same group and same order .*
(g) Nadi	: 1st group. 1,6,7,12,13,18,19,24,25
	2nd group. 2,5,8,11,14,17,20,23,26
	3rd group. 3,4,9,10,15,16,21,22,27
RULE	: *Both should not fall in the same group.*
(h) Gana	: 1st group. 1,5,7,8,13,15,17,22,27
	2nd group. 2,4,6,11,12,20,21,25,26
	3rd group. 3,9,10,14,16,18,19,23,24
RULE	: *Both should preferably belong to the same group.*

Petal 4. Comparison of Malefic Karmic Content: The procedure is as given in chapter 3.

RULE: *The Malefic Content in the female chart should not be less than 75% of the Malefic Content of the male chart or vise-verse for full agreement. If it is between 75% and 50% it is considered average agreement. If it is below 50% there is no agreement.*

Petal 5. Comparison of Planetary Cycles:

RULE: *Lords of the planetary cycles in which the partners are at the time of alliance or would pass through in the future should* *not be mutually in positions $^6/_8$ or $^2/_{12}$ to each other. It is also preferable that future major dasha (Cycles)* changes do not take place within the same year for both.

Petal 6. Comparison of Mutual Position of certain planets:

The chief planets connected with matrimonial or companionship happiness are Sun, Moon, Venus, Mars and Jupiter. From the position of Sun in one chart count to the position of Sun in the other chart. This gives the mutual position. If it is six counting from Sun in one chart then counting from Sun in the other, the Sun in the first chart will be naturally in the 8th position.

RULE: *The mutual positions of these five planets in both the horoscopes should not be either $^6/_8$ or $^2/_{12}$.*

Briefly the comparisons may be classified as:

Petal 1 : Basic temperamental structure agreement based on Mars position.

Petal 2 : Psychological agreement based on Ṛashi (Moon Sign), Rasi Lords, Vashya and Stree Deerga from Petal 3.

Petal 3 : Physical & material agreement based on Dina, Mahendra, Vedha and Yoni.

and Spiritual agreement based on Rajju, Nadi, Gana.

Petal 4 : Karmic content agreement based on evaluating and comparing malefic content in both charts.

Petal 5 : Future situations based on the planetary cycles which the partners would pass through in future.

Petal 6 : Mutual understanding based on the mutual positions of Sun, Moon, Mars, Venus and Jupiter.

Thus we have a thorough study from all angles. They are taken as three Groups. Group one consists of Petals 2 & 3 forming the important study of the psychological, physical, material and spiritual aspects of life. Group second consists of Petal 1 and Petal 4 the basic temperamental structure and karmic situation. Group third consists of Petal 5 and Petal 6 dealing with the possible unfolding of future situations in life and the capacity to sail together through thick and thin.

PART IV

APPLICATION

CHAPTER 13

A Critical Look at The Rules

Let us have a close look at these rules. We note that all the agreements are not possible in any two charts. The system aims at identifying the areas of agreements and the specific areas of disagreement, so that they can together work in a practical way to overcome the same.

For example, according to Mahendra rule, the 7th Nakshatra from one's own Nakshatra agrees, but according to Dina rule the 7th from a Nakshatra is not permissible. Many other combinations also come in conflict with these two rules. It is found that in many cases where Mahendra exists, Dina cannot exist.

If you take Stree Deerga rule, we note that Nakshatras from 1 to 7 counted from the Female Nakshatra are not agreeable. However, the 4th and 7th agree as per Mahendra, but again 4th agrees but 7th disagrees as per Dina.

In the same Stree Deerga we find that it is best if the Male Nakshatra is 15 or more from the Female. So all Nakshatras between 15 and 27 agree. However, many between 15 and 27 do not agree as per Mahendra and Dina.

Let us take Vedha which gives a list of Nakshatras and their opponents. Nakshatra No. 17 disagrees with Nakshatra 2 in this category. However, taking Nakshatra 2 to be the Female Nakshatra and the Male Nakshatra the 17th, counting from the Female Nakshatra to the Male Nakshatra we get the number 16, which is in agreement as per Mahendra and as per Stree Deerga. We can certainly find agreement in Nakshatras by Mahendra and Stree Deerga even when there is disagreement under Vedha.

Thus it can be seen that Nakshatra to Nakshatra there is always some agreement or the other in spite of some disagreements, which is indeed a very happy situation. This in fact means the choice of the areas of agreement and disagreement is yours. If you choose a partner from a certain Nakshatra you will discover that there will be agreement in certain areas, while if you choose another the areas of agreement are different. You have the freedom to set your priorities.

You can make your decisions based on your own values of life. The Vedic comparison system, I should say, makes a broad-minded approach. It is flexible and comprehensive. It places all the cards on the table, with regard to any relationship. The choice is yours. It is only an astrological study and analysis, not a verdict for or against a marriage.

Choosing a life partner, is like making a choice in a super market. You have a large number of different models of the same product. All products are good and each has its own special features. You choose what *you prefer.*

After all between the 27 Nakshatras there are only 729 combinations possible. The results can be tabulated. However, I have not done this because the sages gave us a technique by which, when a person wants to get married to someone, he or she at once knows what areas of disagreement they are likely to encounter and what areas of agreement they will enjoy so that they will be able to decide according to their own sense of priorities in their married life based on social, political, economic, cultural and historical conditions. As such I do not want to present a resultant analytical table as a ready reference as this will psychologically create notions of totally acceptable or prohibited marriages. If a married couple discovers that their Nakshatras belong to the least agreeable category, it may have a very depressing effect.

On the other hand, if one by one the agreements are tested the couple will find some points of agreement and they will be encouraged to work on these to make a success of the relationship and through the areas of agreement find ways and means of neutralizing the zones of disagreement.

Then comes the academically interesting question "Can we have a set of Nakshatras which have the maximum points of agreement ?" It is certainly possible.

EXAMPLE :

Take for example the case where the Female Nakshatra is Uttara Phalguni the 12th where Moon is in Virgo and the Male Nakshatra is Ardra the 6th Nakshatra, in the sign Gemini.

Petals 2 and 3

2 . **Comparison by Moon Sign:** Male Rashi is 10th from Female

a) Hence there is Rashi agreement.

b) Both the Lords being the same planet Budha the Lords are in agreement. Hence Lords of Rashis are in agreement.

c) Vashya : There is also Vashya agreement.

3. **Comparison by Nakshatras** : Female Nakshatra is the 12th, Uttara Phalguni in Kanya. Male Nakshatra is the 6th, Ardra in Mithuna. Count from Female to Male is 22.

(a) Dina agreement	:	Agrees (Full)
(b) Mahendra	:	Agrees (Full)
(c) Stree Deerga	:	Agrees (Full)
(d) Vedha	:	Agrees (Full)
(e) Rajju	:	Agrees (Full)
(f) Nadi	:	Does not agree
(g) Gana	:	Agrees (Full)
(h) Yoni	:	Agrees (Average)

Thus it can be seen that in this particular case there is almost 100 percent agreement as far as Moon sign comparison and Nakshatra comparison. The only disagreement is that of Nadi and both Nakshatras of the female and the Male fall in the same Nadi group which is not acceptable to the Nadi rule. But in the spiritual group, the Rajju agreement is perfect as the two Nakshatras belong to different groups and different order as required by the Rajju Rule.

Hence this combination may be considered one of the ideal agreements under Petal 2 and Petal 3. It may be possible to pick up several such combinations having maximum agreements under different petals.

EVALUATION

Classical Method :

We can also take all possible combinations of Rashi & Nakshatras and evaluate the agreements by giving units and tabulate the results so that we know the most disagreeable pair of Nakshatras as well as check the level of agreement between some Nakshatras.

In fact such an exercise has already been done in a way and some of the Indian language 'Panchangas' (Ephemeris) publish this table. I shall explain first the system of units given in these:

Dina	3	Stree Deerga	1	Yoni	4	Gana	6
Rashi	7	Mahendra	1	Lords	1	Vedha	1
Vashya	2	Nadi	8	Rajju	1	Varna	1 *

The total marks or points given is 36.

Generally, if 18 points are scored the alliance is accepted. We can see from the table of units given that Rashi agreement is 7, Rashi Lords agreement is 1 and Vashya agreement is 2. Hence for Moon sign comparison and agreement 10 points are given. In Nakshatra agreement we have eight types of agreement.

These are: Dina ..3, Mahendra ..1, Stree Deerga ..1, Vedha ..1, Rajju ..1, Nadi ..8, Gana ..6, Yoni ..4, Varna ..1 which total upto 26. Out of this for the three spiritual agreements Rajju, Nadi and Gana we have 15 points, and for the remaining we have 11 points. Thus we can see that the spiritual agreement has been given the maximum points, almost 42% of the total 36 points.

Besides Nadi is given maximum 8 points, next Rashi 7 points so that these two alone secure 15 points.

Next in order come Gana with 6 points, Yoni with 4 points, Dina with 3 points, Vashya 2 point and the rest with 1 point each.

We see that though there are 12 types of agreement, points are maximum for just a few of the agreements.

---

* *A system where zodiac signs are classified as four castes just as they are related to the four elements. I have left out this rule as I consider varna consideration not relevant universally.*

1. Nadi gets 8 points
2. Nadi plus Rashi gets 15 (42%)
3. Nadi plus Rashi plus Gana gets 21 (58⅓%)
4. Nadi plus Rashi plus Gana plus Yoni 25 points (70%)
5. Nadi plus Rashi plus Gana plus Yoni plus Dina plus Vashya gets 30points (83⅓%)

So six of the agreements get nearly 85 percent of the total units, while the remaining get only 15 percent. Since half is the average acceptable, it can be seen that if one has Nadi, Rashi and Gana agreements there is 58⅓ percent of the total units. Even if all the others do not agree. This gives us the indication of the relative importance given to different agreements.

I am not at ease with this system of unit allotment or estimating agreement between charts in this way for the following reasons.

1. The value for each comparison was given under a different set of social circumstances, when the values of life, way of life, attitude to life and even material factors were totally different. Hence this system has to be abandoned altogether or suitably changed and all comparisons made individually to identify areas of agreement and disagreement. Summary disposal is not the modern approach.

2. It has been shown that the rules are such that it is not possible to have all the agreements in any particular case. Also when Rashi agreement exists (units 7) that is the male Rashi is 7th to 12th from female Rashi, obviously the Nakshatra of the male from the Nakshatra of the female, is bound to be more than 15 Nakshatras away thereby automatically ensuring Stree Deerga agreement (units 1). Automatically this becomes an agreement with value 8. It is not a fair way of giving points to the various agreements. It is not advisable to mechanically give these values and arrive at a total figure and make a 'yes' or 'no' decision.

It is important to note that being well aware of this anomaly, the sages gave a list of alternative agreements.

The list is as follows:

(a) If Vashya (2) is not there, it can be offset if there is Gana (6), Rashi (7), Rashi Lord (1) agreements giving a total of 14 points.

(b) If Mahendra (1) is not there see that Rajju (1) and Vedha (1), are there (2 points).

(c) If Gana (6) is not there, see that Vashya (2), Rashi (7), Stree Deerga (1), are there (10 points).

(d) If Yoni (4) is not there, see that Vashya (2), Rashi Lord (1), Mahendra (1), are there (4 points).

(e) If Stree Deerga (1) is not there, see that Rajju (1), Vedha (1), are there (2 points).

(f) If Dina (3) is not there see that Rashi (7) and Yoni (4), are there (11 points).

From this list we note that the attempt is to show that Rashi, Rashi lord, Rajju, Vedha and Nadi are the five most important that can cover the whole range of agreements. But the earlier unit values do not reflect this concept.

3. The psychological basis on which this list of alternatives has been given should be noted. I take only one case to illustrate. If there is no Yoni agreement, there will be lack of physical compatibility and sexual satisfaction. The aim of the system is to hold the marriage together and create conditions that will enable the couple to live together. So it was suggested that Rashi Lord, Vashya and Mahendra agreements should be there. Rashi Lord agreement was suggested to ensure deep emotional agreement between the couple. Vashya ensures extreme cooperation and submission of one to the other. There will be strong desire to give in. Mahendra ensures that the couple has enough material wealth, comfort and physical happiness in many *other* ways. It can be seen that these naturally help the situation and keep the marriage intact through compensation.. The couple

would certainly feel that there is so much at stake to contemplate a break and would soon learn to find substitutes for what they cannot have.

EVALUATION

A Rational Method :

I would suggest the following method for those who are using this system before getting married and want to take the guidance of this system for making a decision. The six petals of comparison may be considered in three groups:

Group 1. Petals 2 & 3. PRACTICAL PATTERNS.
(includes spiritual, psychological, physical and material aspects)

Group 2. Petals 1 & 4. KARMIC PATTERNS.
(Includes the basic temperamental structure and challenges of life)

Group 3. Petals 5 & 6. FUTURE PATTERNS.
(Includes sailing together in time through storm and calm)

GROUP 1. PETALS 2 & 3

We have eleven comparisons based on Rashi and Nakshatra in these two petals. These can be classified into three groups:

1. The spiritual harmony group: Rajju, Nadi, Gana.
2. The Psychological group: Rashi, Rashi Lord, Vashya, Stree Deerga
3. The material and physical group: Dina, Mahendra, Vedha, Yoni.

Each group may be given 12 units. In the first group each gets 4 units. In the second and third group each get 3 units. So the total would be 36 units.

It would be a proper and balanced relationship if each group secured a minimum of 6 points.

This may prove to be a more balanced approach to form a judgment on the basis of comparison by Rashi (Moon sign) and Nakshatra.

I have discussed petals 2 and 3 first because they are important, mathematical, precise and of great importance for comparison. In fact in the ordinary course of astrological comparison only these two comparisons are made and adequate advice is given.

GROUP 2. PETALS 1 & 4

Next in importance is petal 1 because it deals with the position of Mars in both the charts. This should be carefully balanced. There is a tendency among those practicing the Vedic system to apply this rule in a very superficial way. I am of the firm opinion that this comparison of the position of Mars should be clubbed along with the comparison of Karmic destiny, fully described in Petal 4. Just as Petals 2 and 3 form an important set of comparison, so also Petals 1 and 4 together, from another set of comparison. In petal 1 if there is no Mars affliction in both the charts there is agreement. Also if the position of Mars in a Horoscope is adverse and there is similarly adverse placement of Mars in the other Horoscope, according to the rule we should consider the Horoscopes as matching. In petal 4 the karmic contents of both the charts are calculated. If the Karmic content of the female chart is 75 percent or more of the Karmic content of the Male chart or vice-versa, then the charts may be declared as matching.

Regarding the units in Group 2 in petal 1 where we have the comparison by position of Mars we give 6 units when there is agreement. When there is no agreement 0 units are given.

In Petal 4 we compare the karmic contents. If the karmic content of the female is between 75 percent and 100 percent of the male karmic content we give 6 units. If the female karmic content is between 50 percent to 75 percent of the male karmic content we give 0 units. If the female karmic content is less than 50 percent of the male karmic content we give a value of -3. The average acceptable for Group 2 is 6 units.

This allotment of units gives due importance to the basic temperamental structure related to matrimonial life through the energy of Mars and the karmic content in a chart. They are indeed two sides of the same coin.

The various possibilities are:

Petal 1 agrees + petal 4 agrees =	6 + 6 = 12 units
Petal 1 agrees + petal 4 average =	6 + 0 = 6 units
Petal 1 agrees + petal 4 no agreement =	6 - 3 = 3 units
Petal 1 no agreement + petal 4 agrees =	0 + 6 = 6 units
Petal 1 no agreement + petal 4 average =	0 + 0 = 0 units
Petal 1 no agreement + petal 4 no agreemennt =	0 - 3 = -3 units.

This method of evaluating balances the importance of Mars afflicting the matrimonial situation and the intrinsic karmic content. From the values we can see that when there is Mars agreement, even an average karmic content makes the union workable. However, when there is no Mars agreement, there should be full Karmic content agreement.

At the same time we note that even when there is full Mars agreement if there is no karmic content agreement the union proves a difficult preposition.

A real challenging situation exists for the couple when there is no agreement in petal 1 and petal 4. They should identify the strong inner infrastructural personality problems that can reduce the harmony existing in other aspects of their relationship.

GROUP 3 : PETALS 5 & 6

The remaining two comparisons under Planetary Cycles given in Petal 5 and Planetary Aspects given in Petal 6 form the 3rd group of comparison.

In petal 5 we have comparison of planetary cycles. If there is no coincidence of the year of change of Dasha for the couple there is agreement and 5 units can be given. However, if there is coincidence of the change of Dasha in the same year and planets ruling their respective Dashas are in mutually asceptable position in their charts 3 units may be given. If there is change of Dasha in the same year for the couple and lords of the Dasha are not in the mutually beneficial positions ($^2/_{12}$; $^6/_8$) then we should give 0 units.

In Petal 6 we make comparison by mutual planetary positions. We have taken into consideration 5 planets Surya, Chandra, Guru, Shukra and Kuja. We could allot one unit for each planetary agreement. We then have a maximum of 5 units possible under petal 6.

Therefore in Group 3 the maximum possible would be 10 units and the required minimum would be 5 units.
Taking the 3 groups we have :

Group 1. Maximum possible 36 units minimum required 18.

Group 2. Maximum possible 12 units minimum required 6.

Group 3. Maximum possible 10 units minimum required 5.

The total maximum possible comparison units are 58. Minimum required for agreement 29. However, I would advise studying each comparison individually and aim at overcoming the consequences of disagreements by the couple rather than quickly arriving at a mathematical value that either commends or condemns summarily the marriage or union.This would not be helpful. If comparison of charts is made before the partners commit themselves to a relationship, it could probably help them make an enlightened decision. They would not enter a dark alley but a lighted garden path. They would be aware of the potentials and challenges of their relationship. They would know how to tactfully collect the flowers and fruits along their marital path avoiding the pricks of the ever-present thorns.

EXAMPLE 1

Comparision of charts of Female born on 6-2-1928 at 21h-35m G.M.T. (7.2.1928, 3h - 05m standard time) at 16°-57' N. Lat, 82°-15' E. Long and Male born on 26-9-1925 at 18h-05m G.M.T. Female Nakshatra POORVA PHALGUNI, the 11th and the Male Nakshatra is UTTARA ASHADHA, the 21. The count from the Female Nakshatra to the Male Nakshatra is therefore 11.

			Asnd. 12
	Male Chart		Rahu 8
Ketu 8			
Moon 26-51 Jupiter 20		Saturn 19 Venus 19	Mercury 1 Sun10 Mars 6

Jupiter 9		Rahu 23	
Mercury 12	**Female Chart**		
Sun 24			Moon 6.52
Asnd 2 Venus 18 Mars 20		Ketu 23 Saturn 24	

1. Comparison of Mars Position:

In the Female chart Mars is in the 1st sign from the ascendent and Venus. Hence there is affliction of Mars. (30%)

In the Male horoscope Mars is in the 4th from the ascendent and 12th from Venus. Hence there is affliction of Mars. (30%) Since both have Mars affliction there is agreement under Petal1. Units= 6

2. Comparison by Moon Signs :

(a) RASHI: In the Female chart Moon is in the sign Leo, in the Male chart Moon is in the sign Sagittarius. The Male Moon sign is the 5th from the Female Moon sign. Hence there is no Rashi agreement. Units= 0

(b) RASHI LORDS: The Lord of the Moon sign in the Female chart is the Sun and in the Male chart is Jupiter. From the table of planetary friendships, it can be seen that Jupiter is a friend of Sun. Units= 3

(c) VASHYA: The Female Moon sign is Leo and in the table for Vashya Agreement the Male Moon sign is given as Libra. However, in our example the Male Moon sign is Sagittarius. Hence there is no Vashya agreement. Units = 0

3. Comparison by Nakshatras :

(a) VEDHA: According to the Vedha table the Nakshatra of the male, Uttra Ashadha is not opposed to the Female Nakshatra Poorva Phalguni. Hence there is Vedha agreement. Units=3

(b) DINA : The count from the Female Nakshatra to the Male Nakshatra is 11. Dividing this by 9 the remainder is 2. Hence according to the Dina rule there is agreement under this category. Units= 3

(c) STREE DEERGA: Counting from the Female Nakshatra the Male Nakshatra is 11. According to the rule of Stree Deerga it is only average agreement. Units = 1.5

(d) MAHENDRA: The count from the Female Nakshatra being 11. There is no Mahendra agreement. Units = 0

(e) YONI: According to the list of ideal combination, the Nakshatra of the Male and Female are not ideal and the agreement under this category is also average. Units= 1.5.

(f) RAJJU: The Nakshatra of the Female falls in the ascending order of Ooru Rajju and the Male Nakshatra falls in the ascending order of Kati Rajju. Since the order in both is the same though there is differences of Rajju, we may consider there is only average Rajju agreement. Units = 2.

(g) NADI : The Female Nakshatra falls in Sushumna and the Male in Ida. From our illustration we can see that this combination is an imbalanced relationship. Hence there is no Nadi agreement. Units = 0

(h) GANA : The Female Nakshatra falls in Manushya Gana and Male Nakshatra also falls in the same Gana. Hence there is agreement in this category. Units = 4

4. Comparison of Karmic Content.

(Abbreviations : V F = Very Friendly, F= Friendly, O / N=Own/ Neutral, MT = Moola Trikona, Ex = Exaltation, E=Enemy, VE= Very Enemical, Db = Debilitated.)

In each column against each planet the relevant sign position, the relationship and Karmic content value arc given in that order.

MALE CHART

	From Lagna	Moon	Venus
SUN	4/N+ E= E/14	-	12 / N +E = E/14
SAT	-	-	-
RAHU	2/E+ E= VE/30	8/VE/ 120	
KETU	8/E +F= N/64	2/N/16	4/N/16
MARS	4/E+ E= VE/45	-	12 / VE/ 45
	153	+136	+75 = 364

FEMALE CHART

	From Lagna	Moon	Venus
SUN	2/E + F =N / 8	-	2 / N / 8
SAT	12/E + F +N /16	4/N / 16	12 / N / 16
RAHU	-	-	-
KETU	12/F + F =VF/9	4/VF/9	12 / VF/9
MARS	-	-	-
	33	+25	+33 = 91

Percentage of Female Malefic content to Male content
91/ 364 × 100 = 25%

5. Comparison of Planetary Periods :

At the time of birth the Female had a balance of 10 years 5 months and 14 days of Venus Dasha. And the Male had a balance of 5 years, and 11 months of Sun Dasha. Working out the periods we have :

FEMALE		MALE	
Birth	1928 - 2 - 7	*Birth*	1925 - 9 - 26
Venus Balance	10 - 5 - 24	Sun Balance	5-11- 0
	1938 - 8 - 1		1931 - 8 - 26
Sun Dasha	6 - 0 - 0	Moon Dasha	10 - 0 - 0
	1944 - 8 - 1		1941 - 8 - 26
Moon Dasha	10 - 0 - 0	Mars Dasha	7 - 0 - 0
	1954 - 8 - 1		1948 - 8 - 26
Mars Dasha	7 - 0 - 0	Rahu Dasha	18 - 0 - 0
	1961 - 8 - 1		1966 - 8 - 26
Rahu Dasha	18 - 0 - 0	Jupiter Dasha	16 - 0 - 0
	1979 - 8 - 1		1982 - 8 - 26

From the study of the above cycles we can see that there is no coincidence of change of Dasha for them. However, it is significant to note that both run the Dasha of Rahu between 1961 and 1966, when problems could surface.

6. Comparison of Planetary Aspects:

(a) The Sun in the Male Chart is in the 9th sign from the Sun of the female chart. This is good.

(b) The Moon in the Male Chart is in the 5th from the Moon in the Female Chart. This is also good.

(c) The Jupiter in the Male Chart is in the 10th from the position of Jupiter in the Female Chart. This is good.

(d) The Venus of the Male is 11th from the Venus of the Female, this is good.

(e) The Mars of the Male is 10th from the Female which is Good. Hence the mutual planetary positions are all favourable. Units=5

We shall allot units to the various agreements. For this purpose we shall consider them in 3 groups.

GROUP 1. PETAL 2 and PETAL 3.

The Spiritual agreement group :	Rajju	- 2
	Nadi	- 0
	Gana	- 4
	Total-	6/12
The Psychological group :	Rashi	- 0
	Rashi Lords	- 3
	Vashya	- 0
	Stree Deerga	-1.5
	Total-	4.5/12
The Material and Physical group:	Dina	-3
	Mahendra	-0
	Vedha	-3
	Yoni	-1.5
	Total -	7.5/12

Therefore in Group 1 the total is 18 units out of 36 where a minimum of 18 is required.

GROUP 2.

PETAL 1: Comparison of Mars position.

In the Female horoscope Mars is in the 1st sign, from Ascendent & Venus, and in the Male it is in the 4th sign from the ascendent and 1st from Venus. Hence there is equal affliction of Mars in both the charts. We see there is agreement in this. Therefore Units=6.

PETAL 4: Comparison of Malefic Content.

Since malefic content in Female Chart is less than 50% of Male Chart. Therefore Units= -3.
Total for Group 2 = 6 - 3 = 3.

GROUP 3

PETAL 5. Planetary Cycles : Since there is no coincidence the units are 5.

PETAL 6. Planetary Aspects : Since all the Planetary aspects are good, units are 5. Therefore, total units in Group 3 is 10 units, where the maximum required is 10.

Conclusion

From the study of all comparisons we find that in Group 1 there is just sufficient spiritual agreement. Therefore there could be an inexplicable feeling of discontentment and sense of frustration and hostility.

In the psychological group since there is no Rashi and Vashya agreements there is likely to be psychological problems that create a communication gap between them and some amount of hostility.

In the material group since Mahendra does not exist the material position is not likely to be very attractive.

In Group 2 though there is agreement under comparison of Mars position but there is lack of equality of the Karmic content. This comparison indicates there will be a feeling in the Female partner that she has been put to a lot of suffering on account of the misfortunes of the Male partner. Also there is likely to be problem of health affliction of the Male causing frustration and suffering for the Female. This is more so because of the lack of spiritual agreement and consequent affliction of the Subtle Energy Fields of the couple.

Under group 3 there is full agreement, with 10 units. It is this complete agreement in group 3 and the minimum agreement existing in Group 1 that can keep the marriage going as the planetary cycles are helpful.

Facts

The marriage remained intact. The couple had children. When the couple were interviewed in 1986, when the male was 61 and the female was 58, both confessed that they were not at all happy with each other all through and always felt a sense of frustration with tradition only holding the marriage. They were just then constructing their own house and felt their resources were not good enough to have owned one much earlier. The health of the man was unsatisfactory frequently which kept him irritated and generally hostile to his wife, whom he blamed for all his ills.

EXAMPLE 2

MALE BORN ON 09-09-1925	FEMALE BORN ON 20-07-1937
at 17h-10m G.M.T.,	at 9h-25m G.M.T.,
at 16°-57' N.Lat., 82°-15' E.Long.	at 17°-00' N.Lat., 81°-46' E. Long.

		Asnd ☾14°	
	Rashi Chart		☊9°
☋9°			☿6° ☉23° ♂25°
♃19°		♄17°	♀29°

♄12°	☾8°-39'	☋19°	♀5°
	Rashi Chart		☉13°
			☿6°
♃27°	☊19° Asnd 7° ♂3°		

Petal 1 : Comparison of Mars Position :

In the female chart Mars is in the 1st house,the ascendent.It is also the 8th sign from the Moon sign. Hence there is Mars affliction. (40%)

In the Male chart Mars is in the 4th sign both from ascendent and Moon sign, and 12th from Venus. Hence there is Mars affliction. (50%)

Hence for Petal 1 units = 6.

Petal 2 : Comparison by Moon Sign :

(a) RASHI: The Female Moon sign is Aries, and Male Moon sign is Taurus. The Male Moon sign is 2nd from the Female Moon sign. No agreement. Units = 0

(b) RASHI LORDS: The Lord of the Moon sign in the Female chart is Mars.The Lord of the Moon sign in the Male chart is Venus. According to planetary relationship Venus is neutral to Mars.Hence the agreement of the lords is only neutral. Units = 1.5. However combining the above two and if we refer to the table we find the relationship is N4 which is a relationship not acceptable. Units = 0

(c) VASHYA : From the Vashya table corresponding to the Female Moon sign Aries the agreeable Male Moon signs are Leo and Scorpio but the Moon sign in the chart is Taurus. There is no Vashya agreement. Units = 0

Petal 3 : Nakshatra Comparison

(a) VEDHA: The Female Nakshatra is Ashwini. In the Vedha table the Nakshatra opposed to it is Jyeshtha. But the Male Nakshatra is Rohini which is not opposed. Hence there is agreement. Units = 3.

(b) DINA:The count from the Female Nakshatra to the Male Nakshatra is 4. Hence there is agreement. Units= 3

(c) STREE DEERGA: As the count from the Female Nakshatra to the Male Nakshatra is only 4. There is no agreement under Stree Deerga. Units=0

(d) MAHENDRA: The count of 4 falls under the agreeable number for Mahendra. Units = 3

(e) YONI: The Female Nakshatra 1 and the Male Nakshatra 4 representMale horse and Female Snake respectively; Though they do not fall under the incompatible combination given as inimical animals they are not very acceptable.Hence we may consider no agreement under Yoni. Units = 0

(f) RAJJU: The Female Nakshatra falls under Pada Rajju in the ascending order, the Male Nakshatra 4 falls under Greeva Rajju in the same ascending order. This could be considered average agreement under Rajju. Units= 2.

(g) NADI : The Female Nakshatra belongs to the *Pingala* group and the Male Nakshatra falls in the *Ida*. From the illustration on page 93, we note that the relationship between *Pingala* female, *Ida* male is good. Units= 4

(h) GANA: The Female Nakshatra belongs to Deva Gana and Male to Manushya Gana which combination is considered Good. Units 3.

PETAL 4 : Comparison of Malefic content

FEMALE CHART

PLANET	FROM LAGNA	FROM MOON	FROM VENUS
SUN	-	4/F+F= V.F/3	2/V.F/3
SAT	-	12/N+F =F /8	-
RAHU	1/E+E=V.E/120	8/E+E=V.E/120	-
KETU	7/N+F=F/32	2 /F =8	12/F/8
MARS	1/O=96	8 /O =96	-
Total	248+	235+	11 = 494

MALE CHART

PLANET	FROM LANGA	FROM MOON	FROM VENUS
SUN	4 / O / 8	4 / O / 8	12 / O / 8
SAT	-	-	2/F+F=VF/6
RAHU	-	-	-
KETU	-	-	-
MARS	4/F + E =N/24	4 / N /24	12 /N/24
Total	32+	32+	38 = 102

Here we take percentage of Male Malefic content to the Female Malefic content 102/494 × 100 = 21% (approximately)

This is less than 50% and hence there is no equality of Malefic content. Therefore the Units = - 3

Petal 5 : Comparison of Planetary Cycles

Female		**Male**	
Birth	1937 - 7 - 20	Birth	1925 - 9 - 9
Balance of Ketu	2 - 1 - 12	Balance of	2 - 2 - 25
	--------------	Moon	--------------
	1939 - 9 - 2		1927 - 12- 4
Dasha of	20 - 0 - 00	Dasha of	7 - 00 -00
Venus	--------------	Mars	--------------
	1959 - 9 - 2		1934 - 12 - 4
Dasha of	6- 0 - 0	Dasha of	18 - 00 -00
Sun	--------------	Rahu	--------------
	1965 - 9 - 2		1952 - 12 - 4
Dasha of	10 - 0 - 0	Dasha of	16 - 00 -00
Moon	--------------	Jupi	--------------
	1975 - 9 - 2		1968 - 12 - 4
Dasha of	7- 0 - 0	Dasha of	19 - 12 - 4
Mars	--------------	Sat	--------------
	1982 - 9 - 2		1987 - 12 - 4
Dasha of	18 - 0 - 00		
Rahu	--------- -----	Dasha of	17 - 00 -00
	2000 - 9 - 2	Mercury	--------------
	--------------		2004 - 12 - 4

There is no significant coincidence of Dasha change. Hence there is agreement of planetary cycles in general. Units = 5

Petal 6: Comparison of Planetary Positions

(a) The Male Sun is in the 2nd sign from the Female Sun sign. The position is satisfactory.

(b) The Male Moon sign is 2nd from the Female Moon sign. The position is satisfactory.

(c) The Male Jupiter sign position is the same as the Female Jupiter sign position. This is good.

(d) The Male Venus is in the 4th from the Female Venus. This is good.

(e) The Male Mars is 10th from the Female. This is good. All five planetary positions are mutually good. Units = 5.
Grouping the results we have :

GROUP 1. PETAL 2 and PETAL 3.

The Psychological group	Rashi -	0	
	Rashi Lords	- 1.5	
	Vashya -	0	
	Stree Deerga-	0	
	Total-	1.5/ 12.	Only 12.5%
The Spiritual group	Rajju -	2	
	Nadi -	4	
	Gana -	3	
	Total -	9/12.	About 75%
The Material and Physical group	Dina- 3		
	Mahendra-	3	
	Vedha-	3	
	Yoni-	0	
	Total -	9/12.	About 75%

The total units = 19.5 out of 36. Less than 50%

GROUP 2. PETAL 1 and PETAL 4

There is Mars agreement. Hence units = 6.

The Malefic content of the charts are not in agreement hence the units for this is -3.

Therefore, total units under Group 2 is 6-3=3 out of 12.
Only 25%

GROUP 3. PETAL 5 and PETAL 6.

There is agreement of Planetary cycles. The units are 5.
There is agreement of Planetary positions. The units are 5.
Total units = 10.

Analysis & Conclusion

The most significant result of this comparison is the extremely low agreement in the psychological group. There could be serious psychological problems between the couple. In the Material agreements there is lack of physical compatibility. The lack of *Stree Deerga* indicates that they will not be able to enjoy a long marital life.

The Spiritual agreement is good. But there is low *Rajju* agreement. Coming to Group 2, only 25% has been secured. It has been pointed out that the equality of Mars affliction agreement is really effective only if there is a balance of Malefic content. In this case there is no such balance and hence the Mars affliction will have its effects bringing problems or separation.

There is full agreement under Group 3. Future patterns. The evolution of life and circumstances brought over by the future planetary Cycles-Dashas- will help them to atleast understand each others point of view. On the whole it can be seen that there is a great threat for the happy continuation of the marriage and the main reason could be psychological/temperamental and emotional problems. However they may carry on for practical material reasons.

Facts

The couple belong to an orthodox Hindu family and had much cultural, social and family affinity being related to one another as well.

After marriage, serious psychological and temperamental problems created a lot of disagreement. They had 2 children. The marriage broke up. They peacefully parted, dividing their substantial assets including the children!!

The Male however lost everything and led a financially insecure and uncomfortable life with health afflictions while the Female lived in relative financial security, affluence and comfort.In this connection note the low Karmic content of the Male, compared to the female which means he had to experience greater challenges on account of this alliance.

EXAMPLE. 3.

Lady born on 01-07-1961 at 18h 45m G.M.T., 52° 50'N. 0°30'E

		Ven 1°-5'	Mer 9°-55' Sun 16°-21'
Moon 1°-41' Ketu 6°-24'	**Rashi Kundali**		
Saturn 4°-49' Jupiter 11°-44'			Rahu 6°-24' Mars 8°-20'
	Asnd 25°-05'		

Gentleman born on 14-11-1948 at 21h- 14m G.M.T. 51°-30' N, 0°-05' W

	Moon 7°-19' Rahu 10°-47'		
	Rashi Kundali		Asnd 12°-19'
			Sat 12°-36'
Jup 6°-47'	Mars 27°-18'	Ket 10°-47' Mer 13°-52' Sun 29°-17'	Ven 23°-15'

Petal 1 : Comparison of Mars Position

In the female chart Mars is 7th from the Moon and 4th from Venus.There is Mars affliction about 30.5% In the Male chart Mars is 8th from the Moon. There is Mars affliction of 40%. The afflictions are almost equal. Hence there is Mars agreement. Units=6

Petal 2 : Comparison by Moon Signs

(a) RASHI : The Male Moon Sign, Aries is 3rd from the Female Moon Sign Aquarius. There is no agreement. Units = 0

(b) RASHI LORDS : Lord of the Female Moon Sign is Saturn and Lord of the Male Moon Sign is Mars. Mars is a natural enemy of Saturn. There is no agreement. Units =0

(c) VASHYA.: From the Vashya Table, corresponding to the Female Moon Sign Aquarius, the Male Moon sign should be Virgo or Aries. Here it Aries. Accepting the alternative Aries there is agreement. Units = 3

Petal 3. Comparison by Nakshatras:

Female Nakshatra is Dhanistha the 23nd and the Male Nakshatra is Ashvini the first Nakshatra.The Male Nakshtra is the 6th from the female Nakshatra.

a. VEDHA : From Vedha Table there is no opposition between these Nakshatras. Hence there is agreement. Units = 3

b. DINA : Counting from Female Nakshatra, Male Nakshatra is the 6th. There is agreement. Units = 3.

c. STREE DEERGA : Since the count is only 6 there is no agreement and the Units = 0.

d. MAHENDRA : Counting from the female Nakshatra the male Nakshatra does not fall under the agreeable category . Hence Units = 0

e. YONI : Nakshatras 23 and 1 are not in the list of ideal combinations, but only in the acceptable category. Agreement may be considered average Hence Units = 1.5.

f. RAJJU : Female is *Siroh Rajju*. Male is *Pada Rajju*.They are also not in the same order. Hence there is agreement. Units=4.

g. NADI : Female Nakshatra belongs to Sushumna Nadi and Male Nakshatra to Ida. They are not balanced. Units = 0

h. GANA : Female belongs to *RAKSHASA*. Male belongs to *DEVA*. No agreement. Units = 0

Petal 4 : Comparison of Karmic Content and Comparision of Malefic Content.

MALE CHART

	From LAGNA	**From MOON**	**From VENUS**
Sun	Deb 16	Deb 64	Deb 16
Saturn	2/E + F= N/ 16	-	12/ N/ 16
Rahu	-	1/ E+E=V.E/120	8/V.E/120
Ketu	4/N+F = F/ 8	7/ F / 32	2 / F / 8
Mars	-	8/ own/ 96	
Total	40	+ 312	+160 = 512

FEMALE CHART

	From LAGNA	**From MOON**	**From VENUS**
Sun	8/N+E=E / 56	--	2/ E= 14
Saturn	-	12/own/ 16	-
Rahu	-	7/ E+F=N/ 64	4/N= 16
Ketu	4/N+F=F/ 8	1/ F/ 32	-
Mars	-	7/F+F=V.F 36	4/ V.F/ 9
Total	64	+148	+ 39 = 251

Female Malefic content 251. Male Malefic content 512.

251/512 × 100 = 50 % (nearly). Average agreement. Units= 0

Petal 5 : Comparison of Planetary Cycles :

Female		Male	
Birth:	1961 - 07 - 01	*Birth:*	1948 - 11 - 14
Balance of Mars	2 - 07 - 08 1964 - 02 - 09	Balance of Ketu	3 - 01 - 25 1952 - 01 - 09
Dasha of Rahu	18 1982 - 02 - 09	Dasha of Venus	20 1972 - 01 - 09
Dasha of Jupiter	16 1998 - 02 - 09	Dasha of Sun	6 1978 - 01 - 09
Dasha of Saturn	19 2017 - 02 -09	Dasha of Moon	10 1988 - 01 - 09
		Dasha of Mars	7 1995 - 01 - 09
		Dasha of Rahu	18 2013 - 01 - 09

There is no coincidence of planetary cycle commencement for the couple. Hence there is agreement. Units = 5

Petal 6 : Comparison by Planetary Positions:

(a) The Male Sun is fifth from Female Sun. This is good.
(b) The Male Moon is third from female Moon.This is acceptable.
(c) The Male Jupiter is twelfth from Female Jupiter. This is not good.
(d) The Male Venus is fifth from the Female Venus. This is good.
(e) The Male Mars is fourth from Female Mars. This is acceptable.
Since one position is not good the units are 4.

Evaluating the groups.

GROUP 1. PETALS 2 and PETAL 3

The psychological group:	Rashi	:	0
	Rashi Lord	:	0
	Vashya	:	3
	Stree Deerga	:	0
	Total	:	3 / 12

The Material Physical group:	Dina	:	3
	Mahendra	:	0
	Vedh	:	3
	Yoni	:	1.5
	Total		7.5 / 12
The Spiritual group:	Rajju	:	4
	Nadi	:	0
	Gana	:	0
			4 /12

Total Group 1 units are 14.5 for a maximum of 36

GROUP 2. PETAL 1 and PETAL 4.

Petal 1. There is Mars agreement Units = 6
Petal 4. There is only average karmic content agreement.
Units = 0
Group 2 total units = 6.

GROUP 3. PETALS 5 & 6

Planetary cycles do not clash	5
Mutual Planetory positions	4
Group 3 totál units =	9

GRAND TOTAL :	32 / 58
Total Agreement	55 %

Analysis & Conclusion:

In Group 1, the spiritual agreement is glaringly low. This indicates the main problems in the relationship. Practically conflicts could arise because of the spiritual or moral values the partners lay for themselves and for one another. Ethical and moral questions may prove to be the bone of contention. At the end of the chapter 3, petal 3, G on *NADI* the absence of this agreement is said to cause "either one of them will have problems of health, a feeling that the partner is demanding or aggressive or the partner becomes disloyal and promiscuous in some extreme cases" Also at the end of the Chapter 8, petal 3, H. GANA/ Spiritual, page 94, last para I have written "when Deva and Rakshasa are united it is two persons of extreme attitudes trying to work together, it will be constant combat" Apart from this when spiritual agreements are so low it also indicates incompatible subtle energies that may lead one or the other partner to serious psychological and health problems. In any case the psychological group has only 25 percent agreement and the material/physical group just above 50 percent. Psychologically the couple face a great challenge. They should indeed try to rediscover themselves after marriage. A lot of understanding, acceptance, "forgive and forget" approach is necessary. However, materially they could be contented and the marriage could be fruitful with children.

Group 2, with Karmic content agreement value 0, indicates possibility of diverse destinies, unless they work hard to integrate their lives. It indicates a break or separation or divorce. Crisis develops in 1995 when he enters Rahu Dasha as Rahu contributes the maximum Karmic malefic content. Note she enters Saturn Dasha in 1998.

Group 3, has a much better score. This indicates that material or financial issues may not be a problem. They can resolve these easily. Even after a break they can carry on with some responsibilities together, accepting certain ground realities. Though separated they can enjoy some activities of life together.

Facts

It may be of interest to know that in the above example the Lady is PRINCESS DIANA and the Gentleman is PRINCE CHARLES. Facts are now history!

COUNSELLING LINES

When the Vedic astrological system does not support your choice for love and marriage do not blast the system, boost your *Will-Power.*

Astrology is a statistical science.It lays bare the possibilities of the evolution of one's life based on the synchronicity with the planetary patters at the moment of birth. Once the possibilities are known, it is up to the individual to handle the situations whenever they arrive with courage, confidence and a determination to succeed.

Petal 1: If Mars agreement fails.This is by far the most difficult to overcome through will-power. This indicates basic inner personality structures leading to conflict. Since it is difficult for a person to look at himself or herself objectively, it becomes impossible for him or her to accept the problem and try to overcome the same. Most of these problems come because of aggressiveness, short temper, intolerance, anger, a desire to hurt and punish others, to dominate, to command, to assert. These in turn may be the result of deep feelings of inferiority or insecurity, states of constant anxiety, bloated ego, false self-esteem, excessive pride and such other complications. Unless a very deep self introspection is made in a very objective way, one cannot recognize these problems within oneself. But the more difficult task is to overcome these problems. It requires immense efforts, strong determination and Will-Power to overcome these.

Petal 2: Going through psychological therapies or counselling can help both the partners in overcoming psychological problems. It may also be necessary for both the partners to have a frank discussion about their likes and dislikes, their goals and ambitions and their individual fads and fancies.

Regarding material matters similar understanding has to be arrived at regarding, incomes, expenditure, investment objectives, type and nature of professional activities, location of living, preferences of home and environment. Though these may appear to be minor issues, in course of time they blow up to large proportions that threaten matrimonial peace and happiness.

Spiritual incompatibility is another difficult area. Spiritual methods can be very helpful. Fore example, when a couple finds that there is no Rajju agreement between them, it would be advisable that they both perform *Yoga Asanas*. The asanas involving the particular region of the body to which their Rajju belongs would be more helpful. If there is Nadi disagreement the couple should practice *Pranayama* together. It could help them harmonize the energy flow in their Nadis.

If there is Gana disagreement, *Meditation* together at a peaceful place daily at the same time can be helpful for the couple. There are other tantric and yogic solutions, including use of precious gems. But the advice,guidance and supervision of a learned and experienced Guru is necessary.

When there is coincidence of change of major Planetary cycles for the couple, pilgrimage or retreat can be helpful. Taking a long holiday in a quiet place, where there is opportunity for contempl-ation, introspection, and calm planning could be helpful.

If most of the significant planets are in mutual 6/8 or 2/12 positions the need is to develop deep understanding and sympathy for the problems of the partner. Both should be ready to sacrifice their own needs for the sake of the other because this planetary set up creates conflicting interests.

Make the best choice if possible. If the choice has already been made put in the best effort to make it work, once the trouble spots are identified. If you discover you are not the ideal couple do not be upset. You belong to the vast stimulating majority, who get along happily meeting the challenges. Be happy you do not belong to the ideal (?) but boring minority.

PART V

EXTENSIONS

CHAPTER 14

Other Relationships

NON-MATRIMONIAL RELATIONSHIPS

BUSINESS RELATIONSHIPS:

The comparison technique is suitable to be adopted for comparing the Birth Charts of two people who want to join in partnership or join together in some form of association with the object of running a business or a professional activity.

It can be used only when two individuals desire to join in business, as it would be nearly impossible to secure agreement between more than two charts. In comparing two charts follow the procedure:

1. Comparison of Position of Mars.
If Mars is in the 1st, 7th, or 8th sign position from Ascendant of one, it should also be in one of these positions for the other for harmony. If there is harmony give 6 units.

2. Comparison by Position of Moon.
Apply rules of Rashi, Rashi Lords only. Give units 3 for each if harmony exists.

3. Comparison of Nakshatras.
Consider only four Dina, Stree Deerga, Mahendra, and Vedha. For each one of these where there is harmony give 3 units.

4. Comparison by Planetary Cycles.
Here it is relevant to see if both run Malefic Planetary Cycles at the same time. If so there is no agreement. Give 6 units when there is agreement.

5. Comparison by Mutual Position of Planets.
Take into consideration only Sun, Moon and Jupiter. These planets in the Charts should not be mutually $6/8$ or $2/12$. Give 2 units for each planet in mutually acceptable positions so the maximum for

this is 6. The total of these five, if 8 or above indicates a partnership leading to success, continuity and prosperity.

SAME SEX RELATIONSHIPS:

Where two people of the same sex, be they male or female desire to live together in companionship on a sustaining long term basis the suitability or possibility of harmony can be judged using the same techniques.

1. Comparison of Position of Mars.

Compare the same way as in matrimonial relationship. Give 6 units.

2. Comparison of Position of Moon.

Use the same three comparisons Rashi, Rashi Lord, Vashya agreements. Give 3 units for each where there is agreement.

3. Comparison by Nakshatras.

Compare the five, Dina, Nadi, Gana, Stree Deerga, Vedha agreements only and give 3 units for each in agreement.

4. Comparison of the Malefic Content.

Compare as per the normal procedure and give 6 units, where there is agreement.

5. Comparison of Planetary Cycles.

Compare as per the normal procedure. Give units 5, if there is agreement.

6. Comparison by Mutual Planetary Position.

Compare mutual positions of Sun, Moon, Jupiter and Mars if the relationship is between males and consider Sun, Moon, Jupiter and Venus if the relationship is between females. Give unit 1 for each planet in mutually favorable position.

The total, if 24 or above may be considered to help in developing a more harmonious relationship.

EMPLOYER - EMPLOYEE RELATIONSHIP:

Sometimes the relationship between an employer and an employee becomes very important. For example, when someone chooses a person to be a personal secretary or confidential adviser, or security personal or cashier in-charge of his funds, there is need for mutual harmony, trust, and a desire to be loyal and honest on the part of the employee.

1. Comparison of Moon Signs.

Only Rashi and Vashya agreements need to be seen. Give 3 units for each.

2. Comparison of Nakshatras.

Dina, Mahendra, Stree Deerga and Vedha need to be checked. Give 3 units for each in agreement.

3. Comparison by Mutual Planetary Position.

Compare position of Sun, Moon and Jupiter. If not in adverse positions give 2 units per each.

If total is 12 or more the relationship will be harmonious.

GURU-DISCIPLE RELATIONSHIPS:

1. Comparison of Moon Position.

Take Rashi, Rashi Lord and Vashya comparison. Give 3 units for each.

2. Comparison of the Nakshatras.

Take into consideration Rajju, Nadi, Gana. Give 4 units for each in agreement. (see following table to find Rajju, Nadi, Gana agreement straight away)

3. Comparison by Mutual Planetary Positions.

Take into consideration positions of Sun, Moon and Jupiter only and give 1 unit where the positions are in agreement. If the total is 15 (62%) or above the relationship will prove beneficial.

READY RECKONER CHARTS

Petal 2. Rashi + Rashi Lord + Vashya agreements of Female and Male Rashis

MALE MOON SIGN

FEMALE MOON SIGN	♈	♉	♊	♋	♌	♍	♎	♏	♐	♑	♒	♓
♈		2	0	4	10	0	6	12	6	4	4	6
♉	4		4	6	6	4	10	6	4	6	6	4
♊	4	6		0	4	10	4	2	6	4	4	4
♋	4	6	6		4	4	4	8	8	2	4	4
♌	6	2	4	6		2	6	4	4	0	4	6
♍	4	6	12	2	6		4	2	2	2	2	12
♎	6	6	6	2	2	12		2	2	10	4	2
♏	4	6	2	12	6	2	4		4	2	2	4
♐	4	0	4	6	6	2	2	6		2	2	10
♑	6	4	4	4	2	6	6	2	4		10	2
♒	6	4	4	0	4	12	6	2	4	6		2
♓	10	0	0	4	4	4	2	6	6	10	4	

Note: A maximum of 4 units are given for full agreement, 2 units for average, and 0 for no agreement for each comparison.

READY RECKONER
FOR YONI AGREEMENTS EVALUATION
Male or Female Nakshatras

VALUE 3	1	2	3	4	5	6	7	8	9	10	11	12	13	14	15	16	17	18
	24	27	8	5	4	19	9	3	7			26	15	16	13	14	18	17
VALUE 0	13	23	20	21	21	17	10	20	10	7	7	14	1	12	1	12	6	6
	15	25	22	21	21	18	11	22	11	9	9	16	24	26	24	26	19	19

VALUE 3	19	20	21	22	23	24	25	26	27
	6	22		20	25	1	23	12	2
VALUE 0	17	3	4	3	2	12	2	14	23
	18	8	5	8	27	15	27	16	25

Note: If the partner's Nakshatra is not in the row of value 3 or value 0, the relationship is average and may be given a value 1.5

READY RECKONER CHARTS
SPIRITUAL AGREEMENT

The following chart shows which NAKSHATRAS AGREE IN RAJJU, NADI & GANA

FEMALE NAKSHATRAS

MALE NAKSHATRAS	1	2	3	4	5	6	7	8	9	10	11	12	13	14	15	16	17	18	19	20	21	22	23	24	25	26	27
	8	6	18	25	7	2	5	1	14	24	6	26	8	9	1	14	1	3	16	6	6	7	9	3	2	4	5
	15	25	24	26	15	11	22	13	23		25			16	5	19	13	14		25	26	8	16	10	4	12	13
	17				27	20		22						18		23	22	23				17	24	14	11	21	
			24																					23	20	21	

An ideal of 20th Century BC Still valid in 20th Century AD.

Sacramento (California) : For George and Gaynel Couron, love at first sight has lasted nearly 81 years. The couple, who celebrate their 81st anniversary on April 10,has the longest-lasting marriage in the United States, according to Worldside Marriage Encounter, a group offering programmes to improve communic-ation between spouses. "That was the girl for me. I've had her for 80 years, soon to be 81," said Couron, who is 100. "I got the woman I wanted." "I got the man I wanted," his 91-year-old wife added. In 1916, Couron first saw his soon-to-be wife on the sidewalk. He brushed off attempts by his sisters to set him up on a blind date because he kept thinking about that girl on the sidewalk." When he finally did meet Gaynel, at a carnival, she turned out to be the one his sisters tried to match him with. When they met again, he boldly said, "I'm taking you home tonight" and they were soon married. Fourteen children, 43 grandchildren, 75 great-grandchildren and at least 40 great-great-grandchildren later. Couron is surprised as anyone at his long life and his marriage. - AP. The Hindu, Madras. 11.02.97.

MARRIAGE IS A GAMBLE
MAKE THE BEST BET

Glossary of Sanskrit Words

A

Ahamkara : Ego

Ajna : Command; Commanding Chakra in Yoga, situated between the eyebrows.

Akarshana: Attraction.

Angaraka: The planet Mars.

Anuradha: A nakshatra, the seventeenth lunar division in the Zodiac.

Anuraga: Affection.

Apana: One of the five parts of the subtle energy of air we breathe.

Ardra: A nakshatra, the sixth lunar division in the Zodiac.

Arsha Vivaha : Aristocratic marriage, one of the eight kinds of marriages recognized in Vedic society.

Aryan: Respectful person. Also used to indicate a race.

Ashram: The abode of a sage.

Ashlesha: A nakshatra, the ninth lunar division in the Zodiac.

Asura Vivaha: Ungodly marriage, one of the eight kinds of marriages recognized in Vedic society.

Ashwini: A nakshatra, the first lunar division in the Zodiac.

Atma: The inner divine part of the self.

Anubandha: Attachment.

Ayanamsa: Precessionn of the equinoxes

Ayurveda: The Vedic science of health and longevity.

B

Bharani : A nakshatra, the second lunar division in the Zodiac.

Bhava: A house in a horoscope.

Bija: Seed, used for example to mean the root or monosyllable.

Bindu: A point, a unit,

Brahma Vivaha: The Creator marriage, one of the eight forms of marriages recognized in Vedic society.

Brihaspati: The planet Jupiter.

Budha: The planet Mercury.

Budhi: Discrimination.

Bhuta: Element, such as air or fire.

C

Chakra: Wheel, that which rotates. The subtle center of energy in the subtle body mentioned in Yoga.

Chandra: The planet Moon.

Chitra: A nakshatra, the fourteenth lunar division in the Zodiac.

Chitra Paksha: Precession of the equinoxes measured from the position of the constellation Chitra, star Spica 16.

D

Daiva Vivaha: Godly marriage.

Dasha: Planetary period.

Deva: God.

Dhanishtha: A nakshatra, the twenty-third lunar division in the Zodiac.

Dhanus: The sign Sagittarius.

Dharma: That which sustains the Universe; one's duty, a code of life.

Dina: Day. A Principle used in Vedic astrology for comparison of charts.

Dosha: Humors in the body mentioned in the Vedic science of health and longevity. Also affliction.

G

Gana: Group, a classified group. A principle used for comparison in vedic Astrology.

Gandha: Odour

Gandharva Vivaha: Celestial musicians' marriage, one of the eight kinds of marriages recognized in Vedic society.

Gyanendriya: A sense-organ.

Gotra: A social classification like caste.

Graha: A planet

Gunas: Qualities, such as natural instinctive qualities.

Guru: The Planet Jupiter.

H

Hasta: A nakshatra, the thirteenth lunar division in the Zodiac.

I

Ida: Subtle channel of energy on the left side of the body mentioned in Yoga.

J

Jyeshtha: A nakshatra, the eighteenth lunar division in the Zodiac.

K

Kamasutra: Laws of sex, sexology.

Kanya: The sign Virgo.

Kapha: One of the three humors in the body related to the energies of the elements earth and water mentioned in Ayurveda, the Vedic science of health and longevity.

Karma: Action or the fruits of one's action.

Karmendriya: An organ of action.

Katakam: The sign Cancer.

Kati Rajju: Literally the rope at the waist, a classification of the nakshatras for purpose matrimonial comparison.

Ketu : The South Node, considered as a planet in Vedic astrology.

Kuja Dosha: Affliction from Mars.

Kumbha(m): The sign Aquarius.

Krittika: A nakshatra, the third lunar division in the Zodiac.

L

Lagna: The ascendant in astrology.

M

Madhyama Nadi: The central channel of energy.

Mahendra: King of the gods, one of the comparison rules in Vedic astrology.

Makaram: The sign Capricorn.

Magha: A nakshatra, the tenth lunar division in the Zodiac.

Manas: The mind in its functional aspect.

Mandala: A design, an area.

Mangal Dosh: Affliction from Mars.

Manipura: The central Chakra, subtle energy center at the umbilical region mentioned in Yoga.

Mantras: Incantations endowed with energy.

Manushya: Related to the human.

Maraka: Death ; malefic.

Meenam: The sign Pisces.

Mesham: The sign Aries.

Mithunam: The sign Gemini.

Moola (Mula): A nakshatra, the nineteenth lunar division in the Zodiac.

Mrigashira: A nakshatra, the fifth lunar division in the Zodiac.

Muladhara (Mooladhara): The base Chakra, subtle energy center situated at the base of spinal mentioned in Yoga.

N

Nadi: A channel of subtle energy. A principle used in comparison in Vedic astrology.

Nakshatra: Lunar mansion, a division of the Zodiac through which the Moon travels approximately in one day. It covers 13°-20' of the Zodiac.

O

Ooru Rajju: Rope at the thighs. A division of a comparison principle Rajju in Vedic astrology.

P

Pada: A division, one fourth of a Nakshatra, 3°-20'.

Pada Rajju: Rope at the feet. A division of a comparison principle Rajju in Vedic astrology.

Padma: Lotus.

Paisachika Vivaha: Evil-spirit marriage.

Panchanga: Ephemeris, a book giving astronomical data among other information.

Parsva Nadi: The channel on the side.

Pitta: A humour mentioned in Vedic science of health related to the qualities of fire.

Pingala: Subtle energy channel on the right side of the body as mentioned in Yoga.

Poorva Ashadha: A nakshatra, the twentieth lunar division in the Zodiac.

Poorva Bhadra : A nakshatra, the twenty-fifth lunar division in the Zodiac.

Poorva Phalguni: A nakshatra, the eleventh lunar division in the Zodiac.

Prajapatya Vivaha: King-like marriage.

Prakriti: The evolving part of the Divine source, Parvati.

Prana: Life, life-breath.

Punarvasu: A nakshatra,the seventh lunar division in the Zodiac.

Purusha: The non-evolving part of the Divine, Shiva.

Pushya: A nakshatra, the eight lunar division in the Zodiac.

R

Rahu: The North Node, considered as a planet in Vedic astrology.

Rajas: A latent quality in human nature, related to force and action, optimism and courage.

Rajju: A rope. A principle of comparison used in Vedic astrology.

Rakshasa Vivaha: Demonic marriage.

Ravi: The Sun.

Revati: A nakshatra, the twenty-seventh lunar division in the Zodiac.

Rohini: A nakshatra, the fourth lunar division in the Zodiac.

S

Sabda: The sense of sound.

Sahasrara: Brilliance of a thousand suns. The crown Chakra, located just above the head, mentioned in Yoga.

Samana: A part of the subtle energy in the air we breathe in which pervades the stomach region.

Sanskara: Rituals that reform the mind and spirit.

Shani: The planet Saturn.

Shatabhisha: A nakshatra, the twenty-fourth lunar division in the Zodiac.

Sattva: Intrinsic quality in human nature that represents equilibrium, contentment and non-violence.

Sushumna:The central energy channel in the subtle body mentioned in Yoga.

Simha(m): The sign Leo.

Siroh Rajju: The head rope, a division of the principle Rajju use in comparison in Vedic astrology.

Smriti: That which is recollected, such as teachings of a sage recollected by the disciples. Ancient scriptures.

Sparsha:The sense of touch.

Sravana: A nakshatra, the twenty-second lunar division in the Zodiac.

Stree Deerga: Long marital state. A principle used in comparison in Vedic astrology.

Shukra: The planet Venus.

Surya: The Sun.

Sutras: Rules, laws.

Swadhishthana: A Chakra, subtle energy center at the pelvic region mentioned in Yoga.

Swati: A nakshatra, the fifteenth lunar division in the Zodiac.

T

Tamas: Intrinsic quality in human nature that represents inaction, inertia, indifference, and ignorance.

Tanmatra: The essence.

Tula: The sign Libra.

U

Udana: A part of the subtle energy in breath that pervades the upper regions of the body.

Uttara Ashadha: A nakshatra, the twenty-first lunar division in the Zodiac.

Uttara Bhadra: A nakshatra, the twenty-sixth lunar division in the Zodiac.

Uttara Phalguni: A nakshatra, the twelfth lunar division in the Zodiac.

V

Varna: Divisions of Hindu society.

Vashya: Attraction, winning affection. A principle of comparison in Vedic astrology.

Vata: A humor mentioned in Vedic science of health related to the energy of the elements, ether and air.

Vayu: Air.

Veda: Knowledge; ancient knowledge of the sages.

Vedha: Piercing, causing pain, obstruction. A principle in comparison used in Vedic astrology.

Vimsottari: A hundred and twenty, the life expectancy indicated in Vedic astrology.

Vishakha: A nakshatra, the sixteenth lunar division in the Zodiac.

Vishuddha: The Chakra, center of subtle energy situated in the throat region as mentioned in Yoga.

Vivaha: Marriage

Vrishabh: The sign taurus

Vrischika(m): The sign Scorpio.

Vyana: A part of the subtle energy in breath that pervades the whole body.

Y

Yoni: Female sex organ.

Index

Bibliography

Brihat Parasara Hora Sastra (2 Vol.)
Santhanam R.
Ranjan Publications,
16 Ansari Road, Daryaganj,
New Delhi-110 002 (India).

Brihat Samhita (Parts 1 & 2)
Ramakrishna M. Bhatt
Motilal Banarsidass Publishers Pvt. Ltd.,
41 UA, Bungalow Road, Jawahar Nagar,
Delhi-110 007 (India).

Hatha Yoga Pradipika
Swami Vishnu Yogananda
Motilal Banarsidass Publishers Pvt. Ltd.,
41 UA, Bungalow Road, Jawahar Nagar,
Delhi-110 007 (India).

Kala Prakasika
N. P. Subramanya Iyer
The Lawley Electric Printing Press,
KM Hall, Tanjore.

Pranayama
Swamy Kuvalayananda
Kayvalyadhama,
Lonavala,
Maharashtra-410403

Saravali (2 Vol.)
Kalyana Verma, Tr. by Santhanam R.
Ranjan Publications,
16 Ansari Road, Daryaganj,
New Delhi-110 002 (India).